Arthur Griffin
Camera Studies
22 Euclid Avenue
Winchester, Mass. 01890

ARTHUR GRIFFIN'S
NEW ENGL
THE FOUR SEAS

WITH ORIGINAL ESSAYS BY 51 FAMOUS AUTHORS

BLACK AND WHITE PHOTOGRAPHS BY CLAIRE GRIFFIN

HOUGHTON MIFFLIN COMPANY   BOSTON   1980

AND
ONS

Library of Congress Cataloging in Publication Data
Griffin, Arthur, date
New England, the four seasons.

1. New England — Description and travel — 1951– — Addresses, essays, lectures. I. Title. II. Title: New England, the four seasons.
F10.G74   917.4'0443   80–14957
ISBN 0–395–29164–X

Printed in the United States of America

H *10 9 8 7 6 5 4 3 2 1*

THE GLOUCESTER FISHERMAN

This large bronze statue stands on the esplanade in Gloucester, Massachusetts, looking across the harbor to the open sea. It is on your right after you cross the drawbridge on the shore road. Leonard Craske who executed this famous memorial to the fishermen was also a very excellent photographer. I first became interested in photography at a Boston camera club in which he was a member. Gloucester has so many fishing boats tied up to its many wharfs that you'll find it very difficult to come up with pictures that are not too busy. Nevertheless, its narrow streets, its skyline of weathered roofs and spires, the smell of salt air and fish, and sea gulls flying and screeching over your head, give it an interesting atmosphere. You can see Eastern Point light from the statue. This light is the most photogenic light in the Boston area. A heavy granite breakwater runs a few hundred yards to guard the harbor. It is a delightful spot for fishing, picture taking, and picnicking. The black and white photo shows the front of the fisherman statue.

Exposure, 1/25 of a second at f:16. ASA speed 64.

Also by Arthur Griffin

The Boston Book   (with Esther Forbes)
New England
New England Revisited

To Polly, my wife.

She came with a casserole and stayed for dinner.

Book and Jacket Design by Lee Griffin

All Color Photographs Made on KODAK Ektachrome Daylight Film
Color Lithography by Acme Printing Company, Inc., Boston
Color Prints on S. D. Warren Lustro Offset Enamel Dull
Jacket on S. D. Warren Lustro Offset Enamel Liquid Laminated
Endpapers Are Ecological Fibers Rainbow Antique Gold
Composition on Linotype by Arrow Composition Company,
*   West Boylston, Massachusetts*
Binding Cloth Is Joanna Western Mills Natural Finish Kennett Green
*   and Sand Colors*
Smyth Sewn Squareback by A. Horowitz & Sons, Bookbinders

Photographer's Preview

This is your armchair trip through New England's Four Seasons, with some of the foremost writers of this unique area translating my color photographs into words. Each writer was given a print and requested to record such emotion or reaction as the print might arouse, or any comments that lovers of New England would enjoy reading. There are fifty-five individual scenes which show dramatically that *all* seasons in New England are photogenic. They present in full character the most historic and beautiful section of America.

Friends have asked me how in the world I could ever afford to have all these important writers in one book. Well, I just couldn't if I paid them their usual fees. It's really quite simple: all of them are New Englanders who love one or more or all of the six states.

Furthermore, I had the pleasure of knowing many of them from previous assignments for national magazines. Among them Henry Morgan, Arthur Schlesinger, and Maria von Trapp. My first volume included about a dozen of these writers. The ones with whom I didn't have a personal relationship, I secured through Herbert A. Kenny, David McCord, or Houghton Mifflin. It was flattering to me that many busy writers offered to write a characteristic essay.

Now it's a difficult task to select fifty-five pictures from the many thousands I have taken over half a century. I'm a squirrel at heart, for I never throw a transparency away. The most difficult part of selecting these pictures was that every day I thought of yet another print that should be included. I doubt if any photographer could catch New England properly, beautifully, and dramatically in its four seasons, in the space of only a year or two. I visited and revisited some of these locations many times before capturing the values shown in the pictures. In this volume most of the scenes are quite recent, a few old, and some made just in time to squeeze in. Also modern progress has ruined certain subjects. Take Louisburg Square on page 105. Could one ever capture that tranquil scene again without an automobile showing? You'll find in my camera notes that some of these photographs have appeared in national magazines such as the *Saturday Evening Post*. My camera notes also tell of the difficulties I actually experienced in getting the pictures. It's not all wine and roses; but if you love photography, you just take the good with the bad, happy that you are in a profession that beats the outright pursuit of pleasure and is rewarding physically, mentally, and spiritually, and can even be profitable.

I know New England like a book: all the back roads and almost all the inlets and islands along the coast. Over the years I have built up a tremendous file of color transparencies. I've tried to convey the cold, the heat, the beauty, and the uniqueness of New England. The samples in this book are just that — interesting color studies of almost every phase of New England scenery. You can spend a lifetime in the northeast corner of the United States and never photograph as many as you want. All the photographs were enlarged without any retouching, and only a few were slightly cropped. The black and white photographs were made by my dear late wife, Claire. She accompanied me on all my picture-taking assignments over most of the world and was a great help in seeing picture possibilities that I had overlooked. We were a perfect team. Our daughter

Lee, now a free-lance designer in Beverly Hills, designed this volume and my other two volumes of New England, so you can see this is truly a family enterprise.

I tried to help the writers as much as possible with the selection of pictures by giving them a scene familiar to them: Kenneth Galbraith's Court House picture is in Newfane where for years he has spent his summers; Maxine Kumin has four horses; John Ciardi saw many errant golf balls plunge into his pond while caddying at the Winchester Country Club; Joe Garland owns a Friendship sloop; Arthur Schlesinger was partly responsible for the National Seashore Park. Ted Weeks, as a long-time editor of the *Atlantic Monthly,* has walked to work through the Public Garden for more than four decades. Maria von Trapp has skied down the Mount Mansfield Toll Road a dozen times; West Newbury is the town next to John Updike's home; Bill Buckley knows boats; Davis Taylor, a top yachtsman, has sailed in the waters of Martha's Vineyard all his life; David McCord claims to have once run down the long Hammond Trail on Mount Chocorua in forty-five minutes. Taken together the contributions of these articulate New Englanders present a multifaceted and warmly personal portrait of a very special place.

For Camera Enthusiasts

Always have a camera in your car or with you. Keep your equipment down to the minimum you really need, and your photography is bound to improve. Do something new. Change your usual procedure. Break rules. Look for crosslight — not the sun always at your back. This could mean the difference between stagnation and hitting on a new style. Small variations from absolute color accuracy are seldom noticeable and frequently make for better pictures. Remember it's not the camera that takes the picture, it's *you.* Photography is one of the most exciting careers in the world. It is one of the few in which you can conceive, implement, process, and produce from raw film, a beautiful finished product in a short time. Competition is fierce. When in doubt, take the professional's theory that film is inexpensive. Bracket your exposures. Don't feel that you could get better pictures if you only had a new or better camera. With the exception of a Polaroid x70 I haven't bought or exchanged a camera for over twenty years. My smallest cameras are Medalists. These are over forty years old and take a $3\frac{1}{4} \times 2\frac{1}{4}$ transparency. Most of the pictures were taken on 4×5 Ektachrome with the view camera on a tripod. I definitely advise using a tripod whenever possible.

I've been fortunate in my choice of a career that hasn't *seemed* like work. Of course, being mostly self-employed, I have put in far more hours than any employer would have possibly demanded. But for those who accuse me of having it soft, I have a stock answer: "You've no idea how tired my finger gets after a long day of snapping pictures with it, I can hardly wait to stick it around a cold glass of beer to cool it."

Winchester, Massachusetts
September 12, 1980

ARTHUR GRIFFIN

7

Contents

SPRING

by ALLEN H. MORGAN

Spring, more than any other season of the year, epitomizes for me the complexity, the beauty, and the transformation of nature.

Spring in New England is a rebirth of life: literally, in the sense of dormant eggs and seeds spawning their new generations; figuratively, as the first hardy robin arrives on the southwest wind of an early March thaw. Two months or so later a horde of warblers and other tropical winterers sweeps across New England — birds that started their journey from South and Central America at about the same time that the hardy robin left its winter home, perhaps on the New Jersey shore.

The same lengthening of daylight and increasing temperatures that influence birds so strongly similarly affect vegetation and insects. Young Least Flycatchers reared in a nest in this apple tree, whose parents wintered in Mexico perhaps, reach their greatest need for food in mid-June when the insects that nourish them reach their maximum abundance. The honey bees and other insects that pollinate the blossoms so beautifully captured in this handsome photograph emerge from their winter hibernation timed exquisitely with the fruit trees' and dandelions' need to be pollinated. Each nourishes the other — neither can exist without the other. The interdependence and interrelatedness of nature's springtime miracle of rebirth!

Allen H. Morgan is senior vice president of the Massachusetts Audubon Society. He is the recipient of honorary degrees from Bowdoin College, the University of Massachusetts, and American International College, and has received awards from the National Council of State Garden Clubs and the New England Wild Flower Society.

SPRING IN POWNAL, VERMONT

Spring arrives gently. The first thaws usher in the sugaring season — also called the mud season before the hard-top roads were built. Next, tender green shoots on elms and maples appear. Early May opens the fishing season, and pink and white apple blossoms burst forth exuberantly in mid-May with fields of dandelions. In June come wildflowers and lilacs and the smell of rich brown earth turned by the plow. This apple tree is only a few miles from the southwestern corner of the Massachusetts and New York state borders — outside of Williamstown.

Exposure, 1/25 of a second at f:22. ASA speed 64.

An Exceptional Work of Art

by HERBERT A. KENNY

Two things can be said of art. First, that distortion is at the heart of it; and second, that luck is often a major factor in its creation, even though, in baseball parlance, the artist makes his own breaks. Both of these axioms relate to one of the most discussed photographs Arthur Griffin ever took. The occasion was sunset; the place was Horn Pond in Woburn, not far from his home; the season was spring. Viewed horizontally, the picture is a splendid landscape. Turned on its side, it becomes a surrealist masterpiece. The dead tree in the foreground, with its minor branches dropping from a fallen limb and stabbing the still waters of the pond, creates a mirror image, like a magical Rorschach.

Held sideways the picture presents a strange skeletal figure of a nude woman with a disproportionate head like a miniature watchtower, the skull pointed above a narrow band of forehead and two staring eyes flanking dim nostrils. The hips swell sensually; a spider sits at the navel; the swell of the breasts is suggested by a triangle of branch pointing upward toward the throat from which the shoulders slope in a feminine declension. The absence of arms does not detract from the force of the portrait. Stunted branches hold the place of the arms and, with two fronds, which like antennae flank the head, suggest an insect. There are no feet; the figure is cut off at the ankles. A dark line separates the thighs, and directly above, at the region Hamlet might call "the middle of her favors," the tangle of twigs and branches gives at once a hint of realism and the suggestion of a veil. The figure in its entirety might well be a Daliesque conception of the terrifying maternity of the insect world. To the right of the upended figure, the dark trees of the shoreline reproduced in the water create another unearthly figure, befurred and with blazing eyes, a sentinel, heightening the mystery of the whole.

Chosen for its serene landscape, the picture was put on the cover of a telephone directory. The secret portrait (unobserved by Griffin) was discovered by the company's customers. Some were startled, some amused, a few offended, and someone called it "obscene." So many calls came in, the company had to prepare a stock reply. No one seemed to realize that photographic skill and an element of luck had produced a picture that can only be regarded as an exceptional work of art.

Herbert A. Kenny, author of *Cape Ann: Cape America* and *Literary Dublin,* is a poet and historian, and author of ten books, the most recent of which is *The Secret of the Rocks: The Boris Photographs.* His home is in Manchester, Massachusetts, the scene of his most popular children's story, *Dear Dolphin.* He was for many years the literary editor of the Boston *Globe.*

HORN POND
WOBURN, MASSACHUSETTS

This photo was one of the first I selected for my book, and because I wanted a very sensitive essay I called on my good friend Herb Kenny to write it. I have had a great many photos on telephone directories, and when this sunset appeared a few jokers discovered the "nude." Needless to say I was very embarrassed as I had no idea that it was there. It's actually an accident of nature. I've taken thousands of pictures all over the world and this is the first time anyone ever found an ambiguity in any of my photos. Sunsets are the most colorful and beautiful spectacles. I made a limited number of large dye-transfer color prints of this unusual picture and they are rapidly becoming collectors' items.

Exposure, 1/25 of a second at f:11. ASA speed 64.

Morgan Horse Farm

by MAXINE KUMIN

Driving by a Morgan horse farm in spring, you see dozens of foals turned out with their mothers in fields sunny with dandelions. It's an ideal time to start life on the outside after that eleven-month-long gestation.

A foal comes out into the air, front hooves on either side of its cheekbones, like a diver entering the water. Often it will whinny its arrival even before the hind-quarters have kicked their way free of the amniotic veil. The mother will nicker to her baby just as soon as it is on the ground; the foal responds by worming its way toward the mother's voice. You might say it is a reunion for them, together so long, separated in the onrush of labor, now face to face for the first time.

Before it is an hour old, the little one is on its feet, rooting blindly along its mother's flanks in the direction of the milk supply. By the second or third day, that staggering infant-walk has evolved into a steady gait. By the end of the first week, the bare-bones architecture of the foal has begun to fill out. It can run, stop short, turn, and pirouette, executing a harsh ballet. Has nature designed a more aesthetically pleasing young creature?

Close-coupled, sturdy, winsome, with a well-defined head and delicate ears, the Morgan horse is New England's indigenous breed. The line goes back to a small bay stallion owned by Justin Morgan, a Vermont schoolteacher-farmer, who acquired the remarkable colt in 1795. For thirty-two years this stalwart animal served honorably under saddle and in harness. All Morgans descend from him.

HOLDING ON

*Draw me a horse, begs the child
and I draw my dappled filly in a field
grazing on grass as green as
Sherwood Forest. I want to get on, says
the child, so I put him astride
grabbing mane, a little scared but proud
and need not ever take him down
nor she grow older, nor the grass go brown.*

Maxine Kumin won the Pulitzer Prize for her *Up Country: Poems of New England* in 1973. Her most recent collection is titled *The Retrieval System*. Ms. Kumin, author of several novels and numerous children's books as well as six collections of poetry, and her husband live on a farm in Warner, New Hampshire, where all four stalls in their barn are full of horses.

MORGAN HORSE FARM
WEYBRIDGE, VERMONT

I think that this picture says spring better than any other picture I have ever taken. We should all feel this way in spring! Almost two hundred years ago, a schoolmaster named Justin Morgan brought to Vermont a colt of such exceptional qualities that it sired a whole breed known as the Morgan horse. Within fifty years Morgan horses were found in nearly every state in the union. At the state university–owned Morgan Horse Farm (outside of Middlebury), Morgan horses can be inspected and photographed all year. Spring is by far the best time for photographers, for it's then you can find the newborn. This picture shows Nifty, an eight-year-old mare, and her nineteen-day-old foal.

Exposure, 1/200 of a second at f:8. ASA speed 64.

"Some Are Weatherwise, Some Are Otherwise"

by JUDSON D. HALE

Freak weather conditions are standard in New England. In fact, *The Old Farmer's Almanac* was vaulted on to the road to success by predicting "snow and ice" for July 13, 1816. When it actually did snow in Boston on that day, most of *Almanac* founder Robert B. Thomas's 1500 competitors faded into oblivion.

Of course, we all remember the "clattering and spattering" that the *Almanac* predicted for the second week of May 1977. The surprise to everyone was that what was "supposed" to be a rainy spring nor'easter turned into a full-fledged, February-like storm that left us all tramping around the cherry and apple blossoms in some six inches of snow.

Mark Twain said that "one of the brightest gems in the New England weather is the dazzling uncertainty of it," and there cannot be a soul living within our six-state region who wouldn't provide an amen to that. It is indeed fickle, severe, unpleasant (Twain goes on to say New Englanders kill a lot of people every year "for writing about 'Beautiful Spring' ") and, quite often, glorious. Yet, even in the face of the massive evidence of its unpredictability, I would venture to speculate that New England weather does not occur haphazardly any more than anything else in this complex but orderly universe. The earth's trip around the sun takes 365 days, 5 hours, 48 minutes, and 46 seconds. A hundred years from now, that same trip will take one second less. One hundred years' worth of records show that grasshopper abundance rises and falls rhythmically every 9.2 years. For 1300 years, the Nile River floods highest on a regular 17⅓-year cycle.

In short, if all the cycles now being discovered are correct, then even the most cynical skeptic would have to allow that order, regularity, and pattern exist in many types of phenomena — perhaps *all* phenomena — heretofore thought to occur at random.

So it is probable that the freakish, apparently unpredictable weather we experience is actually part of an unbelievably complex series of patterns, the full understanding of which may some day allow us to forecast our weather with accuracy. However, that will in no way preclude our tramping among New England cherry and apple blossoms on snowshoes during the merry month of May.

Judson D. Hale is the editor of *Yankee* magazine and *The Old Farmer's Almanac*. He lives in Dublin, New Hampshire.

WESTON, MASSACHUSETTS

This large green in front of St. Peter's Church is a riot of color in early spring. When it began to snow on the evening of May ninth three years ago, I hoped for bright sun the next day and planned a trip with an early stop in Weston. I had photographed the flowering trees there many times before, and I knew that with a covering of heavy snow I would come home with some very unusual pictures. This was the first time I had the opportunity to photograph flowering trees surrounded by snow.

Camera fans will want to drive a few miles west to Sudbury where they will have at least three good subjects. In the black and white photo is the Wayside Inn. Henry Ford restored the inn — immortalized by Longfellow — and built the Martha Mary Chapel and the stone Grist Mill.

Exposure, 1/25 of a second at f:22. ASA speed 64.

New England Waterfall

KENT FALLS STATE PARK
CONNECTICUT

One of the most spectacular of Connecticut's waterfalls, where the brook is arched by hemlocks, rushes over a precipice in two cascades, down a 200-foot drop within a quarter of a mile. The lower falls (in my picture) have cut their way over white marble steps and have scooped out many potholes in the ledges. Kool cigarettes used one of my pictures of this cool scene in their full-page magazine ads and billboards.

Covered bridge enthusiasts will find a photogenic covered bridge spanning the Housatonic River at West Cornwall a few miles from here. This bridge, shown in the black and white photo, is some 212 feet long and well over 100 years old. It is one of the few remaining covered bridges in Connecticut.

Exposure, 1/25 of a second at f:16. ASA speed 64.

by ROBIE MACAULEY

A waterfall means the coming together of something hard in Nature and something soft. Over the shelf of igneous rock, a stream descends to cut away the softer rock below. And, as is often true in the case of a hard edge joined to a softness and a movement, peculiar beauty comes of it.

New England waterfalls like this one, with their white plumes spilling downward from step to step, remind one of the age and gentleness of New England mountains, and, where they flow, they give the land a voice. Europe had no such voices — except in remote Switzerland or Norway — and when the first explorers came to the new land, they heard a new accent of Nature in it. Friar Louis Hennepin, one of the first white men to see Niagara, called it "a vast and prodigious cadence of water." Even those less vast than the enormous cataracts of Niagara or Yosemite have their own prodigy and their own cadence — and, if you listen carefully to this handsome photograph, you can hear the white voice of New England among the green.

Robie Macauley is a novelist and critic who lives in Boston.

Hazard and Haphazard in Roger Williams Park

by EDWIN HONIG

In the park after the rain, the washed young leaves of early summer wave and glisten when a huge slash of sunlight opens the way before me, as if indicating, like a guiding arm, where I must go to find what awaits me ahead.

Accepting the peremptory signal, I run along the wet black pavement over the bridge, with an occasional rain-licked car slishing by on the road. Still running, I begin to pass the absurdly poised merry-go-round, the unawakened boathouse, and the first tall hedges guarding the misty stream. On my right, enclosed by a planked redwood fence, is the Japanese garden, with its carefully situated footbridge, incised circles of flowers, the freshly upturned loam around painfully defined plants, and the placid midget trees stiffly at ease.

But my jumpy eye seems to want something else — a space of flow and chance, not prearranged things in self-consciously growing postures. So I turn off to watch the ducks in their exploits on the stream. As one dips down, preposterous as a nearly sinking pillow, another flips up, to whirl and sail by as if manipulated by underwater hands. And all around is the faint tide lapping at the shore as if trembling with the zigzagging ducks dipping and turning.

Looking up at the drying trees, I see that no visible order obtains here, but only unlikeness under the wide morning sky; only the insistence, as the poet Wallace Stevens observed, that eccentricity is the rule of nature: now present in the purple splotches of corollas, under great intricate green boughs lifting, by the gray blue muscular waters. Both hazard and haphazard by design and without design. Japanese garden and duck-dotted stream, close and unaiding neighbors.

I scramble to my feet, surprised they can move so straight, being neither rooted in earth nor webbed for paddling water and waddling on the soft shore. I am free to run again but instead I walk, head full of these unavoidable thoughts.

Edwin Honig has been teaching for years at Brown University. He has written many books, mainly poetry. His two latest are *Selected Poems of Edwin Honig* and *Foibles and Fables of an Abstract Man*, a book of prose.

ROGER WILLIAMS PARK PROVIDENCE, RHODE ISLAND

This hilly beautifully landscaped park is known throughout New England for its flower gardens, lakes, and lagoons. It is situated near the center of Providence, and its nearly 500 acres are bursting with color in the spring. The park also boasts a zoo, an aviary, and a deer park. I like it in spring best, for then the flowering trees are begging for photography. This picture was improved with the use of a telephoto lens, which brought the bright azaleas and reflection in the lagoon to the foreground and really made this study.

The black and white photo is of the statue of Roger Williams and, in the background, the Rhode Island state capitol being sketched by a student of the Rhode Island School of Design.

Exposure, 1/50 of a second at f:11. ASA speed 64.

Walking with Hal

by BARBARA DODGE BORLAND

This picture is not of our farm, but Hal and I have owned a farm in Salisbury, Connecticut, since 1952. The farmhouse is not old enough to be important — "just a house-house," as Hal phrased it — but sturdy and strongly built of oak, chestnut, and pine from our own land.

It *looks* like a farm, particularly when the farmer down the road pastures his black and white Holsteins in our fields. We have all the usual outbuildings nestled around the house. But being writers and not farmers, we immediately put them to practical use. Our garage is the old milk house. The woodshed is still a woodshed. The brooder house is full of garden tools. The old chicken house we promptly cleaned out and were delighted to find a cement floor on which we set up our Ping-Pong table. The connecting part of the chicken house became Hal's workshop.

But our big old gray barn with its patina of age, its original stanchions for cattle, and its hayloft is our particular joy. This is a dairy-farming valley, and we let our farmer-neighbors store tractors in the shed on the first floor, store their hay in the hayloft, and use the corncrib for their field corn.

With half a mile of land along the river in front of us, half a mountain in back of us, and pastures and fields all around us on our hundred acres, we knew we had the scope and the beauty we both wanted.

We learned to know each separate part of our land: where we could find showy orchis, wild ginger, bloodroot, and columbine. We climbed up to the top of our side of the mountain, walking on pine needles under second-growth pine that reminded us of the cathedral feeling of the California redwood forests. We learned where the fox lairs were, and the woodchuck dens. We saw deer in our backyard bringing their fawns down to eat windfall apples. We had a partridge in a pear tree and a porcupine up an apple tree. We watched raccoons, possums, wild turkeys, and, in the river, beavers and otters. For a bonus, we discovered that we were on one of the main flyways for migrating birds, north and south.

We never could decide which was the most beautiful season here: apple blossom and lilac time, when our old gnarled apple trees and purple lilacs were in bloom, or Autumn, when the color started from the sumac and woodbine at the river bank and crept up our mountain, which became a riot of changing colors with tawny oaks and green pines as a background. But we welcomed each season in its turn, and walked with it, and gloried in it.

Barbara Dodge Borland, a born New Englander, is the widow of writer Hal Borland. She recently edited *Twelve Moons of the Year*, a selection of his *New York Times* nature editorials published by Alfred A. Knopf.

SALISBURY, CONNECTICUT

This is the loftiest corner of the state and traverses a section unusually rich in natural beauty and historic lore. The Taconic Hills roll away to the north; Lake Wononscopomuc offers lake trout fishing in season and Lime Rock automobile racing. The discovery of iron here in 1732 brought about a statewide stampede that rapidly gathered the fervor of a gold rush. During the Revolutionary War the ironworks were taken over by the government, and cannon and cannonballs for the frigate Constitution *were cast here. This is a most interesting and picturesque section of the Nutmeg State.*

If you are a concert lover be sure to drive over to Stockbridge and take in a Tanglewood concert. These can be very informal, like the one shown in the black and white photo.

Exposure, 1/25 of a second at f:16. ASA speed 64.

Annisquam Harbor Light

by HARRY KEMELMAN

The first lighthouse that a visitor from the interior of the country might glimpse as he drives along the coast of New England is as mysterious and romantic as the ocean beyond it, which, if the visitor has never left the interior of the country, he may also be seeing for the first time. Although some lighthouses are ungainly, spiderlike towers constructed of spreading steel girders that join to clutch a central column in which the beacon is set, many of the older ones are graceful cylindrical masonry towers gradually tapering as they thrust upward to the sky, and add to the aesthetic appeal of the shoreline.

Whilst the landlubber thinks of the open ocean — out of sight of land — as dangerous and menacing, the sailor feels secure and comfortable there, even in a storm. He has room to maneuver. It is when he is in sight of land that he becomes cautious and, if the weather is bad, fearful. For the wind and the tide can hurl him onto the rocks or ground him in the shallows. And frequently there is fog. In its enveloping grayness he can see nothing and is operating blind. As he approaches and enters the harbor, the danger becomes more acute. Even in clear weather the shoreline gives no indication of where the water is shallow, where he might run aground. Annisquam Harbor light helps the sailor approaching Ipswich Bay avoid these dangers. Its white section, visible for sixteen miles, indicates the deep-water channel, while its red section, visible for thirteen miles, warns of the danger of the channel's edge.

The lighthouse's graceful form was not designed primarily for aesthetic reasons. Rather the cylindrical form, which rises forty-five feet above sea level, has the practical effect of exposing a minimum of surface to the force of wind and wave, and its taper lowers the center of the structure's gravity, the better to anchor it to the terrain. Although the intention was purely functional, it adds immeasurably to the charm of the bay.

Harry Kemelman was born in Boston and has lived in Marblehead for the last thirty years. He is the author of the best-selling series of detective stories featuring the exploits of Rabbi David Small, beginning with *Friday the Rabbi Slept Late* and going on through each day of the week to his latest, *Thursday the Rabbi Walked Out.*

ANNISQUAM HARBOR LIGHT
CAPE ANN, MASSACHUSETTS

This lighthouse isn't well known to many people because it's on a winding road in a semiprivate section of Annisquam. Not many tourists actually visit this peaceful little village; they usually head for Rockport or Gloucester. You can frame fabulous sunsets over Ipswich Bay with the round tower in silhouette. The most colorful sunsets and sunrises are over water, which nearly doubles the effect. Quite a few fishing and private boats pass this light on their way into Gloucester Harbor.

The black and white photo is a cold picture of Annisquam Harbor.

Exposure, 1/25 of a second at f:11. ASA speed 64.

The Beholder's Eye

by TIM O'BRIEN

You claim New England's a pretty place? Think again. Oh, it's fine for hiking or camping; it's got all those swell bubbling brooks; it's peaceful and clean and colorful. But, look, when it comes to something truly *important,* like the game of golf, these northeastern states can be downright grotesque. A regular nightmare. Take, for example, the pink and white dogwoods in the accompanying photograph. Lovely, you say? Lush and stately? *Innocent?* Ha! Just for a moment, hop into my golf shoes and take another look. See that road bending so sweetly through the dogwoods? Pretend it's a fairway. Notice how the trees press in on all sides; note that narrow little dogleg angling off to the left; imagine, if you dare, the poor golfer's dismay at having to negotiate his ball through that tightly woven chute. See the problem? That's New England for you. If it isn't dogwoods, then it's pine or beech or maple. Trees everywhere, no clear shot at the pin. And, if trees weren't enough, the golfer's difficulties are multiplied by such hideous hazards as stone walls, gnarled hunks of granite, brambly hedges, ball-gobbling rivers, thickets of sumac that not even a stiff two-iron can cut through. Having grown up on the flatlands of southern Minnesota, I was accustomed to playing golf on courses as wide open and hospitable as freshly plowed cornfields. On the prairie, there is margin for error. You can scramble, you can recover, you can come out of nowhere for that inelegant par. Not so in New England. Here, it's the old Puritan ethic. No straying from the straight and narrow, no wandering from the prescribed boundaries of play, no banana slices, no duck hooks, no dazzling shot to the green from the wrong fairway: there's always a dogwood in your way.

Tim O'Brien is the author of *Going After Cacciato,* a novel that won the 1979 National Book Award.

GREENFIELD HILL, CONNECTICUT

I believe that you cannot find a greater abundance of color in any one small area in the country as in this small hilltop town. This beautiful array of pink and white dogwood is only three miles from Fairfield, and every year there is a church fair during the dogwood season. The entire area is covered with these colorful trees. Note: Tim O'Brien wrote the adjoining essay a few days after golfing with John Updike, Ted Vrettos, and myself at the Winchester Country Club. Some of the fairways are hemmed in with trees. Tim hits the ball a mile but not always straight. He did go into the woods a few times!

The black and white photo is the state capitol in Hartford. The marble and granite structure is so exuberant and electric in spirit that I had to include it.

Exposure, 1/50 of a second at f:11. ASA speed 64.

Maine Peninsulas

by CHRISTINA TREE

Spring blooms are brightest and Down East accents are thickest along Maine's peninsulas. Haunting places, these ragged land fingers stretch seaward from Route 1, dividing coastal waters into half a dozen deep bays and harbors, into numberless quiet inlets.

This was one of the first corners of New England to be settled, and was once an area of intense farming and a spawning ground for famous ships and sea captains. But by the 1880s summer visitors were delighting in the "romantic" landscape: scrub-filled fields and abandoned boatyards.

The visitors came by steamboat and spent the summer in the frame hotels that flourished for a while on the peninsula tips. In Bar Harbor, Abenaki Indians taught ladies to paddle sea canoes, and watched their ancient summer camp become a national park.

The coastal ferries are now long gone. The four or forty peninsulas, depending on how many land spits you count, between Boothbay and Mount Desert are now generally forgotten. Occasionally you hear tell of Castine or Pemaquid, both of them settled since 1630. Friendship is still known for sloops, Port Clyde for a haunted house, and Blue Hill for potters. But summer tourists no longer come by the boatful and fewer each year come exploring by car. Still the paint on house and church is apple blossom white and each spring the flowers bloom brighter.

Christina Tree is the author of *How New England Happened* (Little, Brown) and of *Massachusetts, An Explorer's Guide* (Countryman Press). She is a former assistant travel editor for the Boston *Globe,* and has been writing about New England for some dozen years. She still writes for the *Globe* and is currently co-writing (along with her husband, *Globe* writer Bill Davis) a guide to skiing the winter woods. Ms. Tree and Mr. Davis live in Cambridge with their three sons, Liam, Timothy, and Topher.

EAST BOOTHBAY, MAINE

You can still find lonely apple trees in New England. Yet time was when many a home, in city or suburb, had one or more useful apple trees in its backyard. Now the backyard apple tree is usually dead or unproductive and the boyhood delight of stealing an apple or two has gone with the wind. The boys don't steal apples from the supermarket now, at today's prices that would be grand larceny. I always like to frame pictures. I seldom take a picture without something of interest in the foreground, but I don't often find a frame as good as this old apple tree. Right behind this church is a famous old shipyard. It is still in operation but is now mainly building beautiful sailing ships for yachtsmen.

Exposure, 1/25 of a second at f:16. ASA speed 64.

Our Deer Are Educated

by W. A. SWANBERG

Although Newtown, Connecticut, is only sixty-five miles from New York City, deer abound here. They have a gentility that some say comes from the civilizing proximity of the city and Columbia University. Or it may be due to the fact that shooting them is forbidden, and that some of the neighbors feed them like household pets.

Last fall nine of them were enjoying our Northern Spy windfalls. One of them walked to a nearby pine and with one efficient bite divested it of five feet of woodbine. Then it eyed the zinnias and mums, at which point I opened the door and shouted "No!," forgetting to say please. All of the deer looked at me in utter reproach and trotted off more in sorrow than fright.

Last winter, a hard one with snow and a crust that would support hostile dogs but not deer, seemed a destroyer for the deer. Not at all. Spring came and there they were parading around the back field, grazing like cattle. Beautiful! Someone had fed them well. But what of my vegetable garden? If it escaped the rabbits, woodchucks, and raccoons, what would happen when the deer got in there?

I found out when they *did* get in there, leaving their dainty hoofmarks in charming design. That was all they left. Broccoli, chard, beans, squash, everything — all the delicacies for which I had dug and hoed and spread fertilizer and carried water — gone, all gone.

And there, in the next field, was a doe with a half-grown fawn. She saw me and walked toward me with open enthusiasm. She expected a handout. Regrettably, I forgot my manners. I shouted in indignation and clapped my hands. She trotted away with the fawn, then stopped to turn on me with an expression of disapproval, even contempt. I had been impolite, outraged the amenities.

All of the deer here seem imbued with this same expectation of proper conduct, this upholding of the code. Why, I would scarcely have believed it if I hadn't seen it with my own eyes, but the other day a doe came to the back door, prettily raised a forefoot and knocked.

That's the way things are here in Newtown, and the vegetables we get come from the roadside stand.

W. A. Swanberg lives in Newtown, Connecticut, and is the author of several notable biographies. He won the Pulitzer Prize for *Luce and His Empire* and the National Book Award for *Norman Thomas: The Last Idealist.*

DEER IN CONNECTICUT

I have traveled some 25,000 miles a year for many years all over New England and have not seen much wildlife. When I have seen deer, by the time I grabbed a camera, all I could get was the rear end disappearing through the trees. This doe was evidently stunned by my appearance, and I was able to get a couple of pictures before she took off. The only bear I met was while taking a picture of Mount Katahdin in early spring. My camera was on the tripod when I heard a rustling behind me. Suddenly a big black bear appeared. I left my camera and slowly backed to my car and quickly got in. The bear sniffed the camera and walked off. I was completely ignored!

The fawn in the black and white photo strayed into a farmer's yard and was so young that it had to be fed from a baby's bottle.

Exposure, 1/100 of a second at f:8. ASA speed 64.

Atlantic Sunrise

by EDWARD ROWE SNOW

New England's coastline holds an almost universal appeal for all Americans. Arthur Griffin has caught the ocean in a moment of serenity in this view of sunrise calm with the boats at rest "away down Maine." This quiet, peaceful scene is in direct contrast to the tempests and hurricanes that often sweep the New England area leaving death and destruction in their wake.

In all ages and climes the treacherous sea has been the inspiration and terror of man, and this is shown in music, art, and literature. The ancient Greeks were fascinated by the adventures and voyages of discovery as they sailed over oceans, often to their death. The Bible has countless references to the sea, and Shakespeare's *Tempest* is a gripping drama of the violence encountered on the waves. American writers and poets also tell of storms and tragedies on the ocean.

Scores of lighthouses guarding the rocky ledges along the New England coast have had their part in lessening maritime disasters, and the sheer beauty and fascination of these watchmen of the night will always remain for us to enjoy, even though modern devices such as radar, sonar, radio, television, airplanes, and helicopters have greatly cut down the tragedies.

New England abounds in tales and stories of shipwreck, piracy, death at sea, coastal burnings, marine battles and Civil War encounters, all of which enhance the unique heritage of this section of the United States.

The Albion Cooper pirates, who were captured and executed more than a century ago, vie for importance with the unusual sixteenth-century Dixie Bull, whose complete story should be given a high place in New England's pirate history. Men like John Winthrop and William Bradford, stern New Englanders as they were, both wrote effectively about Dixie Bull. "God destroyed this wretched man."

Tragedies of the sea and shore are equaled by catastrophies on land. The fire that destroyed most of Portland in 1866, more than ninety years after the awesome earlier conflagration in the same area, was a double blow to this great city, which has been visited with lesser holocausts from time to time.

Pirate treasure has been discovered often in New England, and there are scores of incidents regarding the finding of gold, including the priceless coins hidden by the Indian Madockawando in the Castine area.

Edward Rowe Snow, called by the *New York Times* "the best chronicler of the days of sail alive today," was born in Winthrop, Massachusetts, and now lives in Marshfield, Massachusetts. Throughout his career his paramount interest has been the study of pirates, treasures, lighthouses, shipwrecks, and ghosts. It is generally agreed that he knows more about his subject than any other living person. Mr. Snow is in the process of publishing his ninety-fifth book.

SUNRISE
PROSPECT HARBOR, MAINE

You are quite a way Down East when you reach Prospect Harbor. This area of Maine is unspoiled, and it is not at all known to the average motorist. It is a top area for all sorts of camera studies. Prospect Harbor adjoins the Schoodic Peninsula, which is part of Acadia National Park. From Schoodic's rocky shore there is a beautiful view of the ocean and Cadillac Mountain at Bar Harbor across Frenchman Bay. At Schoodic Point the ground swells come rolling in against the rocks after a storm and the gulls actually eat out of your hand, as they are in the black and white photo here. On the eastern side of Schoodic Peninsula is Wonsqueak Stream, locally called One Screech. It is said that a jealous Indian became angry with his squaw, took her out in his canoe, and threw her overboard. Before the waters closed over her she gave one screech.

Exposure, 1/25 of a second at f:11. ASA speed 64.

SUMMER

by ROBERT B. PARKER

Summer in New England is earned. We accomplish it through proud endurance. And we accept it as proper wage for the winter we have once again outlasted. Fish are jumping, quail whistle about us, school is out. And while living may not, in fact, be easy, the cinch of limitation is loosened. We know it will tighten in a while. We know, perhaps better than others, the implacable alternations of life — in the effulgence of July, we do not forget January. This is the moral condition of New England. The alternate contraction and relaxation of our spiritual frame has made us sinewy (and stiff, perhaps). We are grateful. We do not long for endless summer. We know that death is the mother of beauty, and we know that only those who have stood beside the frozen water and shivered in the wind can take the full measure of sunlight and locust hum and fish moving in the deep eddied pools beneath the falls.

Robert B. Parker lives in Lynnfield, Massachusetts. He is a professor of English and the author of several novels. He received the Edgar Allan Poe Award for his novel *Promised Land*. When not teaching and writing, he plays softball and lifts weights.

WELLS RIVER, GROTON, VERMONT

I've been passing this series of little falls for quite a few years without knowing they were just out of sight off Route 302, a mile west of the village of Groton. Lake Groton, the source of Wells River, is only a few miles away in Groton State Forest, a splendid area in which to camp out. I found these boys in the house across the highway. One had a fishing rod, and the other rod was in my car. (I have always carried props in the car — before men's shirts became colorful, Claire dyed a few old white shirts in bright colors to put on farmers, fishermen or other folks whenever I needed a spark of color.)

Exposure, 1/25 of a second at f:16. ASA speed 64.

The Dash and Roar of Infinity

by ARTHUR M. SCHLESINGER, JR.

The yellow dunes squat in the sun, defending the white sands against aliens from the interior. Beach grass, sparse and straggling but sharp as a knife, bristles on the frontier. But the sea glitters and calls, the invasion mounts, paths break through the dunes and the soft sands fall under human occupation. Thoreau saw the great beach of Cape Cod in its boundless innocence. "The solitude," he wrote, "was that of the ocean and the desert combined." Today, at least in the genial months, the beach more closely resembles Grand Central Station.

There are those who like crowded beaches. As for me, I think that three on a beach is a crowd and glower at unoffending interlopers a hundred yards away. This is wrong. Ways must be found to reconcile nature and democracy. John F. Kennedy, who loved the Cape, supplied one in the Cape Cod National Seashore, where families are welcome and the fast-buck blight is not. Families after all belong on beaches. One remembers so many sun-drenched afternoons, the children hunting shells or building castles in the sand or plunging with ardent cries into the surf to the rhythmic dash and roar of the waves; then, as the sun sets, gathering driftwood for the fire of early evening.

Crowded or empty, in tranquil sea or in savage white-capped storm, the beach endures. It cleanses the spirit, reflecting and absorbing every human mood. In its union of endless sky and endless water and endless sand, the beach is the nearest thing to infinity we are likely to encounter in earthly existence.

Arthur M. Schlesinger, Jr., is Albert Schweitzer Professor of Humanities at the City University of New York and winner of the National Book Award for *Robert Kennedy and His Times*.

CAPE COD NATIONAL SEASHORE

Until recently, Cape Cod's natural and historic beauty was preserved by individuals and the towns and the Commonwealth of Massachusetts. The establishment of the Cape Cod National Seashore in 1961 now permanently ensures federal protection. No longer threatened are the wild beach, heath, forest, and ponds in one of the last expanses of uninterrupted natural lands along the Atlantic. Cape Cod National Seashore ultimately will embrace some 27,000 acres of land and promises to keep intact the ancient charm and beauty of the old Cape for future generations. I made this picture of Nauset Beach from the Coast Guard Beach area.

The black and white photo of the wrecked fishing boat was made on this same beach a few years ago.

Exposure, 1/100 of a second at f:16. ASA speed 64.

Sailing Toward Europe

BOSTON FROM NAHANT

by HENRY CABOT LODGE

My boyhood was spent in Nahant, that rocky promontory that sticks out toward Europe, and is about ten miles from Boston. The boats that were very common in Nahant in my boyhood were Nahant (or Swampscott) dories. These were good sea boats. They had two sets of oarlocks, two sets of oars, a leg-of-mutton mainsail and a jib of suitable size. There was a dory club in Nahant — I believe it still exists — and under its auspices we had dory races. Then there were the "star" boats. I did not own one, but sailed one with the late Malcolm W. Greenough. I remember one sail from Nahant over to the Eastern Yacht Club in Marblehead, which we thought was quite a sail in those days.

Later most of my sailing centered around Beverly and Manchester and I had a variety of boats, some sail and some outboard. Boats are fascinating. They are a lot of trouble, but I believe they are worth it. In recent years I had a twenty-two-foot Mako with two outboards. I could easily leave Manchester, go through the Annisquam Canal and go up the Castle Neck River to enjoy the marvelous seawater that comes in over the hot stones when the tide turns and provides a most wonderful swim because the water is clean and fresh and warm there. The view of the white sand dunes at Ipswich is beautiful to watch while swimming. I believe there is nothing more beautiful in North America.

Henry Cabot Lodge has been a U.S. Senator; an ambassador to several countries, including South Vietnam; a vice-presidential nominee; representative to the United Nations; special envoy to the Vatican; journalist; author; a much-decorated major general; and chief U.S. negotiator at the Paris peace talks. Mr. Lodge was unanimously commended and thanked by the U.S. Senate for his Vietnam service. He lives in Massachusetts and is currently writing two books and lecturing on U.S. foreign policy and national politics.

When Henry Cabot Lodge wrote in his adjoining essay "My boyhood was spent in Nahant, that rocky promontory that sticks out toward Europe, and is about ten miles from Boston," I imagine that he was remembering the view he had of Boston while sailing in Nahant waters. Of course the Boston skyline then was not at all this outstanding. The black and white photo shows the white sand dunes he passed while sailing up the Annisquam Canal in the background. Nahant and Little Nahant were sold in 1730 by the Indian chief Poquanum for a suit of clothes, two stone pestles, and a jew's-harp. Steamboat service to Boston in 1817 caused Nahant to develop rapidly as a fashionable watering place. I brought the Boston skyline into good view with a 15-inch telephoto lens.

Exposure, 1/50 of a second at f:14. ASA speed 64.

Summer in Winchester

by JOHN CIARDI

From 1930 to 1933 I caddied at the Winchester Country Club, remaining a fish caddie to the end. I didn't mind the work, or toting the bag, but I had no eyes for the ball. There were blueberries to look for. There were chokecherries — astringent but habit forming — to pick and cram into the mouth. In season I pinched the flower sprout of chickory and went home with a pocketful to sweeten that night's salad. Mushrooms popped up among the trees where my golfer's ball remained forever lost. Later the milkweed pods swelled day by day, to pop fragrantly open and then drift off as lint. An eggshell under a tree was a command to look up till I saw the nest. A horse chestnut stumped out of its prickly pod was a topaz, a useless one, but polished bright. On weekends during school the apples lit.

And there was water. A deep slow brook ran just behind the hut where the caddies waited. It was a universe of things, much like the tide pools in the rocks of Lynn Beach. Pollywogs wiggled in, changing almost before my eyes. Tiny silver fry darted through it. Queer dark bugs bumped along the bottom, and queerer ones skated on the surface, while dragonflies hummed, forever louder than the caddie master's call. He learned to leave me to the last, or to send me out with grandma duffers who couldn't hit a ball far enough to lose it, but said after every thirty-five yard dribble, "Well, at least it was straight." I liked them. Their bags were light, their patience was easy, and their golf was nothing even they could take seriously. If I said I knew where to find Indian pipes, or lady slippers, or white trillium by the pond, they were willing, often as not, to let the long-ball men play through while they took a look. They were only out for a walk. As I was.

When asked to send some biographical information, John Ciardi wrote: "I was born in the North End of Boston — literally, for I was midwived at home, in the top flat on Sheafe Street, where the Old North Church tower did for our kitchen clock. But we moved to Medford early on — 'out in the country,' as my cousins put it. And it *was* almost country then. We kept hens and, before Easter, a lamb. One of our neighbors kept two cows, and another bees. The Mystic River was just across the street, still mostly clean then.

"It's all gone now — the fields closed out by ugly houses, row on row, and the river an open sewer. I am an overweight ex-professor who stopped professing to find time to write: fourteen books of poetry, a dozen of children's poems, some collections of essays, a translation of Dante's *Divine Comedy,* a collection of limericks with Isaac Asimov, and, to be published next year, *A Browser's Dictionary,* the first in a proposed series on the origins of words and phrases."

MORTON'S POND, WINCHESTER COUNTRY CLUB, MASSACHUSETTS

This lovely pond between the second and third fairways was made by Bill Morton, an early wildlife enthusiast, as a bird sanctuary and a retreat for Canada geese on their way south. His charming Irish country estate is in the background. It's not at all unusual to have flocks of half a hundred geese in for a month or more, freeloading on Bill's supply of grain. Quite a few "birdies" are made on the third fairway as geese get in the way of line drives. The pond also attracts the errant balls of wild golfers off the bordering fairways. I didn't dare golf when I first joined the club because the vistas from the course were so beautiful that I just couldn't help feeling guilty chasing that white ball when I should be off taking pictures. Even now, at times, it's a toss-up if I'll golf or take pictures.

The black and white photo shows a regatta on the Mystic Lakes, which you can see from the golf course.

Exposure, 1/25 of a second at f:22. ASA speed 64.

The Magic of East Corinth

by RALPH NADING HILL

Among many other similar villages in the clefts of Vermont's narrow valleys — hamlets that as Robert Frost observed "can't in nature grow further" — East Corinth has become one of New England's most familiar scenes. Each year a covey of photographers alights on its gentle hills to rediscover its visual and symbolic charms. It has never been captured more faithfully than here in the shaft of light that has already passed over the darkened ridge.

Since the rendering of a landscape must provide the illusion of depth by way of a richness of detail that diminishes in size from forefront to background, it behooves the photographer to seek a subject that extends all the way from his feet to the horizon. The Green Mountain lowlands offer numberless such opportunities, but in all the variousness of their many white and red wooden towns none fills the bill as admirably as East Corinth.

But of course there are other than technical reasons for pictorial pilgrimages there. It was this kind of scene that moved William Allen White to declare that Vermont is every American's second home. Home is the word that comes nearest to explaining what has become known as the Vermont mystique, for it suggests a herbage of stability and security that is elsewhere at a premium in the rootlessness of the present day. The greater the complexity and anonymity of the urban and suburban sprawl, the more endearing the fundamental values of a natural backdrop.

That is the appeal of a state that has had the wisdom or good fortune or both to safeguard the trappings of its traditions, and of the rural past, the heartland of the American experience.

Ralph Nading Hill, a lifelong Vermonter, has written many books about northern New England, for which he has received honorary doctorates of letters from Dartmouth and the University of Vermont. He has been active in historic preservation for over three decades. As president of the Shelburne Steamboat Company he operated the 220-foot sidewheeler *Ticonderoga*, now a national landmark, during its final years on Lake Champlain, and was instrumental in its overland voyage to the Shelburne Museum, of which he is a trustee.

EAST CORINTH, VERMONT

Vermont offers an infinite variety of moods and subjects for photographers and artists, any season of the year. The pleasing combination of mountains and valleys and colorful countryside — like those in this scene from high up on a hill — has brought many artists to Vermont. The day I took this picture was very cloudy; I had to wait for the sun to break through. I have always followed the advice of the old New England saying, "If you don't like the weather in New England, wait a minute," and quite often the sun has popped through. On other days I have waited for hours — and a few times days — for the proper light. And, of course, the long waits were on assignments when I had to get the pictures.

The black and white photo shows farmers pitching hay. While I was climbing the hill, Claire was taking pictures of the farmers haying. (You can see the hay-wagon in the right corner of the green patch of hay in the color photo.)

Exposure, 1/25 of a second at f:16. ASA speed 64.

The Friendship Sloop

by JOSEPH E. GARLAND

What is there about the plodding, nodding Friendship sloop, close-reaching so sturdily, so comfortably, against the summer sou'wester off the coast of her native Maine, that gives such a friendly tug to the heartstrings of the sailor? Something leaps within me, as if I were in the presence of some vibrant eternal verity, when I chance upon one of these doughty gaff-riggers out of another age, whether she is pounding by me close aboard, main topsail quivering, bone in her teeth, lee rail agurgle, or hull down to seaward, a flash of white on the horizon, or riding placidly at her mooring in some pine-girt cove . . . nor do I much care whether she's one of Old Man Morse's originals, her ancient planks held on with haywire and roofing nails, or a sleek aseptic plastic reproduction.

Well, I admit to partiality. I am the master of a first cousin to the Friendship, a Gloucester sloop of fifty adventurous years once owned by the fabled Howard Blackburn, a trifle less handsome but quite as able; and wherever we sail we get friendly hails along the way like some familiar veteran of the Boston Marathon, bringing up the rear but getting there all the same.

What is there about these compact ghosts from the graveyard of sail that elicits such sentimentalism? Fairness of face and figure? Yes, but they are jolly old maids jigging over the deep compared with the breathtaking ballerinas that are today's aerodynamic triangles, pirouetting across an icy sea. Efficiency? Hardly.

No, I guess we devotees of the Friendships and their breed have to admit that the root of our passion, like all true love, is slightly irrational. Yachts these old timers are, but they don't *look* like yachts and they don't *sail* like yachts because originally they were fishing sloops, designed for wresting a living from the sea. Best of all, they don't *feel* like yachts, and so, as we up anchor, raise main and jib, and head out for an afternoon's run up the coast, when we should be minding the store or fashioning a paragraph, fantasy permits us half-sheepishly to imagine that we are ploughing the sea for something more than pure pleasure, for some such worthy objective (what utter rationalization!) as preserving a vibrant eternal verity of maritime lore, or tugging at a passing heartstring.

Thus assuaged, conscience reluctantly slips overboard, blends with yon frothy wake and disappears astern — and the rest of the day is ours, old boat and thee and me!

Mr. Garland is a Gloucester writer and the author of ten books, including *Lone Voyager*, the life of Howard Blackburn; *Eastern Point*; *The Gloucester Guide*; and *Boston's North Shore: Being an Account of Life Among the Noteworthy, Fashionable, Wealthy, Eccentric and Ordinary, 1823–1890*, published by Little, Brown in 1978, the sequel to which is in the works.

FRIENDSHIP SLOOP RACES FRIENDSHIP, MAINE

These races are very informal and are held every July. Sloops come from all over the East Coast for this annual regatta. This is one sailing race at which photographers can easily get pictures. All you need is a boat and you can cruise along with the sloops for your shots. The Friendship sloop was designed as a fishing boat small enough to haul traps among the ledges, yet fast and powerful enough to set trawls far offshore. When the marine engine supplanted fishermen's sail, yachtsmen found Friendships comfortable, lively, lovely little vessels. In Friendship and the adjoining villages you can find plenty of fishing nets drying on rickety wharfs, and at times the shores are lined with piles of lobster traps. Andrew Wyeth has summered and painted in nearby Cushing for most of his life.

Exposure, 1/200 of a second at f:11. ASA speed 64.

Spring Tides

by THOMAS BOYLSTON ADAMS

The tides of sea join man to the cosmos. The shore dweller can feel it. Put your hand into the pulling water of the sallywinder, the little salt river that flows twice each lunar day out to sea and back from it, and you are in touch with the universe.

Where the sallywinder turns through the salt marshes, all nature senses — as it senses nowhere else, not in the high mountains or on the plains, or on the great ocean itself — the silent forces that rule life. The sun forever leaves one half the earth in moving darkness; the tides promise the light's return.

Twice each month the tide springs. At the new moon and the full moon it rises out of its usual banks and floods the marshes. The beaches disappear or become no more than the narrowest edging to the encroaching sea. The sea, a vast dark monster, stirred by invisible, irresistible forces, licks its way into the land. It seems it will not stop. The lobster buoys turn bottom end up, pulled nose down by their lengthening ropes. The boats that lay helpless, immobile on the sand wake to life and frolic on the rising flood, looking down with some surprise at the stakes that tether them. The wharves creak and strain as the water seeps and lifts at their foundations. A loose board floats away.

Someday will the tide just keep on springing?

Mr. Adams has been writing for many years for Boston newspapers. His first printed piece was titled "The Old Two Masters" and celebrated the last working sailing vessels on the coast. He came to the sea at the age of four weeks and has swum in it and rowed and sailed on it ever since. In between he has engaged in various business enterprises and politics, has been president of the Massachusetts Historical Society, and is treasurer of the American Academy of Arts and Sciences. The Nixon administration honored him by putting him on its enemies list.

TURBOT'S CREEK
KENNEBUNKPORT, MAINE

The coast of Maine begins in Kittery. It is less than two hundred and fifty miles as the sea gull flies. If you could straighten out all the bays, rivers, and coves and make a straight line out of them, it would be well over three thousand miles. And this would not include a couple of thousand islands. I made this picture many years ago so don't expect to see this setting again. Over the years most of the area behind the dory has been filled with gravel and a few weekend cottages have been built.

If you are a lover of old Colonial houses, you'll find Kennebunk a gold mine for architectural subjects. The black and white photo is the much photographed Wedding Cake House.

Exposure, 1/25 of a second at f:11. ASA speed 20.

Welcome to Menemsha

by DAVIS TAYLOR

England has its Eddystone Light. Menemsha has its Bell Buoy. For those at sea or on the beach, the Bell does however have a unique something all its own — a haunting, weird, hushed sound on a windless heavy foggy day, a violent loud bang on a turbulent nor'west or nor'east day and a silent sentinel loneliness on still moon-lit nights. Amateur sailors beware in heavy weather! On land, the curvy ups-and-downs approach to this unmatched dockside village is charming, and please, all drivers, slow down and respect its peacefulness.

Through the years this little fishing port has retained its identity with the past. The wharfs where the fishing boats tie up have a crustiness about them that is un-beatable. The inlet, Menemsha Pond and Quitsa Pond, have that something special that comes from salt marshes on the east, little coves on the southwest, and a high bluff and white sandy beaches on the west and north — they are so perfect even a full moon or a rising sun can hardly improve upon them.

The houses seem to snuggle so well into the landscape that man has spoiled it hardly at all. Menemsha has a famous herring creek where in early spring an un-wary bass fisherman standing up to his waist casting, may be passed by a "friendly" six- or seven-foot shark!

If you are going to cruise into the pond, be "self-contained," the harbor master is on the job. Menemsha, too, has something unusual — two thieves of Baghdad: one an islander, the other an off-islander.

The post office–store, picturesque coast guard station, and shops make this little spot on Martha's Vineyard something very special.

Davis Taylor was publisher of the Boston *Globe* for many years, and is now chairman of the board of Affiliated Publications, Inc.

MARTHA'S VINEYARD
MENEMSHA, MASSACHUSETTS

Martha's Vineyard, a triangular isle off the elbow of Cape Cod, measures less than twenty miles from east to west and ten miles from north to south, with its high-est point 311 feet above the sea. The island was per-manently settled in 1642, and became a whaling cen-ter in the eighteenth century. This small island offers so many possibilities for pictures that if you are not care-ful you'll run out of film. Edgartown with its old colo-nial houses, Gay Head and its very colorful clay cliffs, peaceful rural scenes, and this old fashioned fishing vil-lage of Menemsha. My picture was taken quite a few years ago and I believe that a few of the fishing shacks have been destroyed by storms since.

Exposure, 1/25 of a second at f:8. ASA speed 20.

Meditation in Maine

LAKE MOOSELOOKMEGUNTIC MAINE

by LEE KINGMAN

Blazing down on mountains and lake, the incandescent sun is as hypnotic as a mandala — that symbol of centering that meditation seeks. The longer one contemplates this sun, the more it seems to have focused on itself the attention of the clouds, the sky, the earth, and the water — and they are all concentrating on a dramatic dénouement to the end of day. It would be a fitting time for mediation or, without conscious effort, for letting the sense of solitude that seems to arise from this view of deep woods, untroubled waters, and distant mountains renew a weary spirit.

Yet encountering a phenomenon such as a brilliant sunset can be as exhilarating to the eye and as exalting to the spirit as music is to the ear. Sunsets over cities and suburbs are accompanied by sounds, which, if they are as inappropriate to their glory as car horns and jet whines, must be consciously tuned out. Sunsets over remote Maine lakes may still be observed during moments of soundlessness — in the pure luxury of quiet. Yet, for those who long to hear those rare sounds once more, there is always the hope that there will be loons calling — breaking the silence with their wild arousing cries.

Lee Kingman is the author of twenty-six books for children and young adults, and is the editor of books about art and literature in children's books, such as *The Illustrator's Notebook*. She and her husband, Robert Natti, live on Cape Ann by the edge of a now water-filled quarry, Blood Ledge. The famous fisherman's statue, *The Man-at-the-Wheel*, rests on a block of green granite that was cut from Blood Ledge quarry.

It is not difficult to make beautiful sunset pictures when one is at the right place at the right time. You usually have to plan this beforehand. I had this high vantage point in mind for some time. This view of the lake is from Route 17 in the wilderness country along the New Hampshire frontier. This large lake is one of the many lakes, ponds, streams, and rivers in this region and is famous for its fighting trout and landlocked salmon. This spot is over 2100 feet above sea level — you can see forever from here. One shouldn't be too stingy with film in such situations. Take several shots, altering the exposure when you are not exactly sure of the correct one. Compared with coastal Maine, this area is very quiet and peaceful. There are several resorts and motel-type accommodations. One very good inn overlooking Rangeley Lake has an interesting golf course with magnificent vistas.

The black and white photo is a view of Saddleback Lake a few miles from Rangeley.

Exposure, 1/50 of a second at f:8. ASA speed 64.

Hi Tide, Low Tide

by FRANCIS E. WYLIE

Herring, clams, and high tides are three things that Lubec, Maine, has in abundance.

The herring fishery isn't as big as it once was but in a good year the sardine canneries can't keep up with the glittering harvest brought in by boats from weirs and seines. Lubec has nearly 3000 acres of tidal flats — plenty of room for clams, though they don't grow as fast as those in warmer waters. The flats are exposed by tides so low that when high tides come they may be under twenty-five feet of water.

All of that water rushing in from the Gulf of Maine brings dangerous eight-knot currents through the Quoddy Narrows between Lubec and Campobello Island, just 250 yards away, beyond the Canadian border. Some sixty years ago, Dexter P. Cooper, an engineer living on the island, watched the tides sweep into Passamaquoddy and Cobscook bays and calculated that the millions of tons of water could produce millions of kilowatts of electricity. He interested Franklin D. Roosevelt, a summer resident, in a scheme to dam the Narrows and build other dams in Passamaquoddy Bay to impound the tides and produce power. After becoming president, Roosevelt gave a go-ahead on the project but got cold feet when it appeared the cost would be $65 million. Work was stopped.

The scheme didn't die, however, and in recent years the energy crisis has made it more attractive. The Army Corps of Engineers studied a plan to use only Cobscook Bay, perhaps running dams from Lubec to Eastport, less than three miles away. But, although the project would be much smaller than the original Passamaquoddy undertaking, construction costs have gone up. A guess is that the price would be $1.5 billion — more than twenty times as much as the cost that scared Roosevelt. It would save millions of barrels of oil but even at today's fuel prices would not be economically attractive. Unless, or until, the energy crisis gets worse, Lubec and its tides, herring, and clams are not likely to be affected by a power project.

Francis E. Wylie, a freelance writer and author of *Tides and the Pull of the Moon*, lives in Hingham, Massachusetts.

HI AND LOW TIDE, LUBEC, MAINE

During the mid-1960s, residents of this easternmost town in the United States were hopeful that the proposed renewal of the Passamaquoddy Power Project, delayed for three decades, might come to pass. This project was to take advantage of the massive tides, among the highest in the world. This picture will convey a rough idea of the height of the average tide. In the background is Campobello Island, former summer home of Franklin D. Roosevelt. The island is now connected to the mainland by a bridge from Lubec. I was very lucky that both boats in my first picture were still there for the second picture, taken six hours after the first.

Nearby is West Quoddy Head light, shown in the black and white photo. This light is called the Barber Pole light because of its wide red and white stripes.

Exposure, 1/25 of a second at f:22. ASA speed 64.

The Swan Boats of Boston

by EDWARD WEEKS

City parks are for pleasure. Boston's Public Garden is a gentle park and the pleasure comes from the tulip beds' swatches of color that proclaim the spring, from the roses that follow, and from the all-summer contrast of shade and sunlight under the great trees. The action is provided by the Swan Boats, which made their first voyage with passengers in the lagoon in 1877, and have been circling the tiny island ever since.

The Swan Boats were designed by Robert Paget, and the fleet has been owned and operated by his descendants to this day. Robert, an opera buff, was inspired by Wagner's *Lohengrin,* in which a knight of the Grail crosses a river in a boat drawn by a swan. For propulsion Paget consulted Colonel Albert Pope who was beginning to manufacture bicycles. The present boats, which are larger than the originals, carry twenty passengers, including presidents; the late Admiral Richard Byrd, who took his grandchildren for a ride on his return from Antarctica; Shirley Temple; French and British sailors on shore leave; and "Sally Mallard." Sally was a stowaway who hatched her brood of thirteen ducklings secretly in the stern of a Swan. On a bed of straw, with an apple carton for cover, they toured the Lagoon for a month.

Paul Paget, of the fourth generation, is the present Admiral and Navigator of the Swan Boats; his fleet consists of six, the newest of which he helped his father build in 1958. He constantly receives offers from abroad to purchase one of the fleet or their design, but in his opinion the boats were built exclusively for Boston and should sail only in the Public Garden.

The year before he became editor of the *Atlantic Monthly,* Edward Weeks settled on Beacon Hill. Daily, for more than four decades, he has walked through the Public Garden, mulling over difficult manuscripts and worshiping the trees.

THE PUBLIC GARDEN
BOSTON, MASSACHUSETTS

The Boston Public Garden is twenty-four acres and the adjoining Common forty-eight more. This is a very large stretch of green to find in a major city. They have been together more than a hundred years. One hundred years ago the water still came up over present-day Arlington Street. Planted with rare trees, and gay with flowers and the Swan Boats in summer and skaters in winter, the Public Garden is much loved by Bostonians and tourists. It hardly seems like spring in Boston until the flowers begin to bloom there. All through the flowering season as soon as one species has stopped the next begins — bulbs first, then fuchsias, geraniums, and heliotrope. The Garden is wonderfully photogenic in all the seasons, but don't neglect the Common.

Exposure, 1/100 of a second at f:11. ASA speed 64.

Troy on Aquidneck

by JOSEPH GERARD BRENNAN

Summer is Newport's season. Cool breezes from Narragansett Bay and the open Atlantic beyond have refreshed generations of Americans since pre-Revolutionary days when Southern planters enjoyed the old town's mildness of air and tolerance of slaveholding. Summering there, South Carolina's John C. Calhoun wooed his future wife. Even before the Civil War, bankers and businessmen from Boston and New York were sending their elegant womenfolk away from the summer swelter of their townhouses to the shade of Bellevue Avenue and the sun of Cliff Walk. The James family settled in a corner of Spring Street while young Henry studied drawing with John La Farge, haunted the Redwood Library, and stored up memories of Newport's "far-away little lonely, sandy coves, rock-set, lily-sheeted ponds, almost hidden, and shallow Arcadian summer-haunted valleys with the sea just over some stony shoulder."

To Thornton Wilder, Newport was a second Troy, not one Rhode Island town but nine superimposed on Aquidneck Island's southern tip. Today Trinity Church, where philosopher George Berkeley preached in Queen Anne's time, looks down across a park cleared by restorer Doris Duke to the wharfs where fishing boats captained by sons of Yankees, Portuguese, and Italians unload their catch to feed visitors from Philadelphia, Wichita, and Los Angeles, weary from their trudge through the palatial mansions of Ocean Drive that once housed the Four Hundred. The oldest Jewish congregation in the nation still meets at Touro Synagogue; the Navy Training Command remembers the two Commodore Perrys, Oliver and Matthew, as well as Mahan, Luce, Spruance, and Stockdale, legendary heads of the Naval War College on Coaster's Harbor Island. The Newport Jazz Festival has moved to New York, but the America's Cup races are as constant as the Gothic tower of St. George's school, landmark to yachtsmen and fishermen alike.

Some say Newport's loveliest months are September and October, others are loyal to May and June before the high summer crowds invale. But even in November when the bay turns gray black and the chill wind hustles in off the Atlantic, Newport keeps its spell — of a kind that has made lively entrepreneurs and tired wanderers alike exclaim on coming to it, "This is the place. Let's stay here."

Joseph Brennan, teacher and writer, now lives most of the year in Little Compton, Rhode Island, across the Sakonnet Inlet from Newport. His most recent book is *The Education of a Prejudiced Man*.

OLD NEWPORT, RHODE ISLAND

There are two distinct Newports: the first is the old center now being restored; the second is the opulent Newport with its great estates on the famous Ten-Mile Drive, which connects the large mansions along the shore, and winds nearly straight south from the center, swings west along the shore, and winds back to the center again. It would take pages to list the many points of interest and historic buildings to see and photograph in Newport. Among the pictorial subjects are the Touro Synagogue, probably the oldest synagogue in America, Trinity Church, Old Colony House, and the many large mansions.

The black and white photo shows The Breakers, the most striking and magnificently appointed of Newport's "cottages." Many of these mansions are now open to the public. You can actually spend a few days going on house tours here.

Exposure, 1/25 of a second at f:22. ASA speed 64.

Cape Cod

by HENRY MORGAN

This is the time of the year on the Cape when there's just a hint, just a thin suggestion of a tingle in the air. Soon, some of the boats in the harbor, birds at heart, will be flying south to escape the winter. Others will be hauled ashore, stripped of rigging and sails, to doze in their cradles until the spring. The commercial fisherman will stay where he is, more than likely, working right through the cold — unless ice locks him in for a few days.

Those of us who live here year round feel our blood running a little faster. For us, native and wash-ashore alike, this is the best of times. As the air gets sharper we feel a strange mix of relaxation, because the summer people are gone, and elation, because now it's all ours. There's no one to disturb our miles and miles of glorious beaches and sometimes, when low tide and sunrise coincide, we get dressed early in the new day and then, in the chilly dawn, walk a few miles along the flats to watch the tide come in. The long ridges of water crest and foam and tumble and dissolve and rush in a soft susurrus up to our feet. A sliver of sun — there it is! — and through the salty air, over the bustling water, a new day comes to Cape Cod.

We don't fill in marshland anymore. What may look like weeds to you is the beginning of life to us. Most everybody knows by now that the marshes are where most of our seafood chain begins. It has been estimated that in nutrient value to man, an acre of marsh is worth about six of corn. And, of course, they are the feeding grounds for millions of birds who stop off here on their two-thousand-mile journey to the forests of South America. But that's not why we love them. It's their color. The scrub pines set the basic tone year round but it's the marshes that, as winter draws on, give us the pale mauves, the misty violets, and the vague purples that delight the eye with their ever-changing palette.

The airy, salty tang, the gentle colors, and the living water — this is the Cape we know.

Mr. Morgan has been a humorist on radio and television for years. He lives in Truro, Massachusetts, about a mile from where, he says, "the Pilgrims first stole corn from the Indians."

58

SUNSET AT STAGE HARBOR CHATHAM, CAPE COD

This sunset came up very suddenly. Usually with a clear sky you wouldn't expect to get such a tremendous impact. I used my telephoto lens, which makes the glowing ball of the sun appear to be much larger; it also provides a narrower angle of view that eliminates undesired objects that could be distracting in the foreground and sides. Unless you really know the Cape, especially from Orleans down to Provincetown, you can become very confused about where the sun will set. Look at this section on a map and you'll see what I mean. The first rule for getting good sunsets is to choose a proper vantage point from which to take the picture, preferably across an expanse of water.

The black and white photo is of one of the few remaining windmills and is in nearby Eastham.

Exposure, 1/25 of a second at f:16. ASA speed 64.

FALL

by ANNE BERNAYS

A New England fall has the sort of reality summer will never have. Summer is an idyll; lush, throbbing, lazy, it delivers promises and fantasies spun in February. Fall puts an end to the dreaming. But while it is an end, it is also a beginning. Things start up once more. You regather and regroup.

As for Nature in fall, she's in a tricky mood. The fields pulsate yet with the sound of cricket and cicada. The trees are round and full as they were in mid-July; the ponds lie there misty, warm, seductive. One day camouflaged as summer, fall can easily toss off this disguise and appear as prophet: cold, wet, angry. And on the third day she is revealed in a crystalline brightness, wherein each leaf is saturated with red the color of flame, and the sky with blue the color of imagination.

If there's a sadness in the death of summer, this dying carries in it, after all, the embryo of spring.

Anne Bernays is a Cambridge novelist — her latest novel is *The School Book*. She teaches writing in the Harvard Extension Program.

MYSTIC LAKES, WINCHESTER, MASSACHUSETTS

The mist-shrouded vista and haunting beauty of this fall scene is something very few people see or, when they do see it, seldom bother to capture on film. I pass this lake most weekend mornings while driving to the Winchester Country Club for early morning golf. I always have a camera in the car, and many mornings I stop to get the sailboats at anchor. Those stops make me a bit late for my golfing foursome and while rushing to the first tee I'm always greeted with, "Shooting pictures again. Making money on our time." Usually I compensate for my tardiness by letting the guys win a few bucks ... On cold fall mornings heavy fog and mist arise from warm bodies of water. Mist allows beautiful studies — sun makes the picture and it's best to shield the direct sun with a branch or something. It'll also improve composition and emphasize background. Imagination is the key to good photography.

Exposure, 1/50 of a second at f:11. ASA speed 64.

Morning Glorious

by JERROLD HICKEY

My earliest memory of fall foliage was roundabout — and upside-down. It was an hour or so after dawn on Armistice (now Veterans) Day, and a friend and I were attempting an assault on the fence near the bears' cage in Norumbega Park on the Charles River in Newton, Massachusetts.

The sun hadn't yet hit the river and a sort of foggy steam lay about three inches thick on the water. The sun hadn't hit the high metal fence either, and it was covered with a thin layer of ice from the unthawed frost. (Hilary couldn't have boosted the Sherpa Tensing over that slippery surface.)

The sun still had some work to do before it could be considered daytime, and since we had some time to kill and the river was surprisingly warm, we stripped and slipped in the water between two overhanging bushes.

The water was palpably soft, and floating with the current we were invisible in the wispy layer of fog. Then, in what seemed like a flash, the sun hit the river and the fog disappeared. The surface was completely still, and looking toward shore I saw, as if below me in the dark water, a buried valley of lambent incandescence. Looking above the bank I saw what at first seemed to be, in that ethereal atmosphere, a reflection of what the water held.

Of course, reality intruded. The sun rays slanted at an increasingly higher angle, backlighting first the branches and then the tops of the fiery trees on shore. It was a glorious sight. But the magic moment had passed.

I still consider the watery part of the world the only vantage point from which to watch the seasons change. And I live on that river today, half a mile from the spot of my memory.

Jerrold Hickey, formerly a book and magazine editor and currently under cover as a bureaucrat, moonlights as an author's agent and starlights as a poet.

EARLY FALL ROAD SCENE IN MASSACHUSETTS

A camera opens more doors for you than any other gadget. It's your passport to long-lasting friendships. With a camera in your hand you can approach pretty girls without the guilty feeling that they might take you for a dirty old man on the make. For instance, driving up this road I saw this vista of early fall foliage, but with the road bare I didn't bother to stop. Around the bend I came upon these photogenic damsels. A few minutes later I had them in the picture and later sent them prints for their kindness.

In late summer and early fall camera enthusiasts can find wonderful pictures at the many fairs. The black and white photo is of the popular rock pulling contest.

Exposure, 1/25 of a second at f:22. ASA speed 64.

A Certain Reverence

by DAVID McCORD

There is a mountain radiant in the sun,
With half New England under its granite head;
A forest shouldered where the deer still run,
And at its foot the Indian lies dead.

Proud Chocorua, straight out of Euclid, splendid from every angle! Examine all those husky shoulders and ask yourself: What other mountain in North America surpasses her in grace, proportion, profile, mass, cathedral dome? Chocorua: the elderly climber's paradise, the camera's flawless model of a mountain.

Exactly sixty years ago I had seen from a distance but had not yet climbed easy Wachusett and popular Monadnock, and I had heard about Chocorua. All other mountains, including the Presidentials, Emerson's Mansfield, and Thoreau's lonely Katahdin, were but icons like the magic names of London, Oxford, Paris, Athens, Rome. I had seen the Poconos; the Rockies; Mount Shasta in California; Mount Pitt in southern Oregon; Hood, Saint Helens, Adams, and Mount Ranier from our front porch north in Portland. But save for Pennsylvania's Big and Little Pocono, none were friendly mountains.

So it happened that in 1919 I climbed Chocorua for the first of many times. I climbed it with my Harvard classmate John Hodgdon Bradley, for whom today's oldest fossil known to man is named. That gradual ascent along the shady, murmurous Brook Trail took a curious, fearful turn as we neared the summit. For we had early overtaken the first man either of us had ever seen wearing shorts: a young Swiss, fresh from the Alps. We joined him; and as we emerged above treeline, he carefully considered the majestic dome and then suggested that we abandon the trail and climb the sheer east chimney wall. Neither John from Iowa nor I from Oregon knew anything of rock climbing; and I have never wanted to know more than I learned that morning on a scary hand-and-toe-hold quasiperpendicular ascent. I had milked some unfortunate cows as a boy, and my hands were strong, though my knees were weak. I had always loved to look up at the sky, but never so much as for those twenty dreadful minutes! I gaze on this spectacular view of Chocorua with a certain reverence. But it was another old friend, the late Le Grand Cannon, Jr., who paid the enduring tribute to Chocorua in his 1942 novel *Look to the Mountain*, a Book-of-the-Month Club selection, and still deservedly popular.

David McCord edited Arthur Griffin's *New England Revisited*. His last two books were nominated for the National Book Award. *One at a Time,* his collected verse for children, won the first National Council of Teachers of English Award, 1978. Latest verse: *Speak Up,* 1980.

MOUNT CHOCORUA
NEW HAMPSHIRE

About the first person I contacted to write an essay for this book was David McCord. He was in my first volume, New England, *and edited* New England Revisited. *This is a view of Mount Chocorua that tourists seldom see, yet it is only a few hundred yards off Route 16. When you reach the town of Chocorua, turn left on Route 113 toward Tamworth and after you cross the Chocorua River you'll see this vista on the right. Mount Chocorua as seen through the famous birches back on Route 16 (in the black and white photo) was always one of our favorite vantage points. Unfortunately heavy ice storms have destroyed the old familiar birches. The state of New Hampshire planted some new birches a few years ago, but it will be many years before they are large enough to frame Chocorua. Why didn't they transplant larger birches?*

Exposure, 1/25 of a second at f:16. ASA speed 64.

The Sea

by NATHANIEL BENCHLEY

Say the words *New England,* and one person will think of a white church spire and a village green; another will see a covered bridge or the Vermont hills in autumn; and still another will conjure up a farm along the Connecticut River. For me, the words evoke the sounds and smells of the sea, and the storms and the fogs that make life along the New England seacoast a good deal like living on an actual ship, subject to the whims of the weather.

The sea is always a presence, and can be sensed even when it cannot be seen. A cool wind, carrying with it a faint smell of brine; a gentle breathing sound at night, or the hollow pounding of waves against rocky cliffs; or simply a feeling of distance beyond the last line of trees; all these indicate the presence of the sea, and, for anyone who wants further proof, a short walk will usually bring it into view. If it is hidden by fog, it can still be detected by the small sounds it makes in contact with the shore, or if at night by — as Matthew Arnold put it — the grating roar of pebbles flung up the high strand. It is, in short, impossible to live near the sea without being aware of it, and without feeling the atavistic pull it has on the descendants of those who came from it.

Nobody knows for sure who was the first European to see the New England coast. It might have been the Vikings, it might have been a band of Irish monks, or it might have been some unknown fisherman, lost in a fog and blown south from the Grand Banks. As far back as the tenth century a man named Bjarni Herjolfsson, looking for his father who'd gone to Greenland, cruised along the Labrador coast without ever setting foot ashore, and considering his navigation he might have been the first to spot what later became known as New England.

To cruise the coast nowadays, if fog or haze obscures the cities, is not too different from what it was like in Bjarni's time, with the obvious provision that radar and loran make the navigation considerably more accurate. The forests and coves of Maine could, by a stretch of the imagination, be thought of as virginal, and once the details of civilization have been blotted out you are left with the sea. Pods of whales appear, blow puffs of vapor, and slide out of sight to reappear and blow again in a lazy rhythm; seals and dolphins and unidentifiable creatures rise briefly and then vanish, and the man and his boat are set back in time a thousand years.

Nathaniel Benchley was born in Newton, Massachusetts, and since 1922 has been a resident of Nantucket Island, first as a summer visitor and later as a year-round convert. He is the author of a number of books, both for children and adults, the most recent of which is *Sweet Anarchy,* a novel about the secession of a mythical island from the mainland.

BALD HEAD CLIFFS
OGUNQUIT, MAINE

Sunrise pictures have a powerful impact in color. And if you take one you'll get a scene that few people see, for how many camera fans arise at that ungodly hour? If you have never taken a sunrise picture, you are missing one of the best of all pictures. You should remember that sunrises have a tendency to come up fast and change unexpectedly, so be prepared with your camera on a tripod and plenty of film at hand. The cliffs here are the highest until you get down east to Monhegan Island.

Be sure to stop at Perkins Cove (black and white photo), an artists' hangout with interesting gift shops, restaurants, and a picturesque harbor with excursion boats. Winslow Homer was one of the many famous painters who painted this coast. Ogunquit has a very long, hard sand beach, and the water is very cold. That's the only fault that I have with Maine, the water is just too damn cold.

Exposure, 1/25 of a second at f:16. ASA speed 64.

New England's Brooks

by RICHARD WILBUR

New England's brooks, streams and small rivers have incited many to poetry, starting with Anne Bradstreet's meditations on the Merrimack — in whose tributary the Concord Emerson discovered a symbol of the flow of Being. Frost's "West-Running Brook" handsomely ponders one of our lesser watercourses. I suppose that I could stand beside the brook in our woods and rehearse such meditations, or think up something of my own about the great symmetries of the creation, of which the watercycle is one. But such thoughts are best worked out in the study.

The thing to do with a brook, I think, is to climb or descend it, now scrambling along the bank, now jumping across from rock to rock, now crossing back over on a fallen tree trunk. That way you are always within the infinitely changing music of it. The music changes because at every step the water's behavior changes; it will pour from a stony lip and drill into the surface of a wide pool, then roll over a broad ledge in a hushing sheet. In the long run, too, there are great changes, as when a torrent trundles down through the dark of hemlocks and is dammed into a small pond, its surface scarved perhaps with spawn or pollen; then there will be a raucous, glittering little waterfall, and another downhill jostle until the pitch lessens and the water rambles out, temporarily, into a swamp full of hellebore and marsh marigold.

We know what thrives by brooks, and in them; what swims in them, strides on them, skims over them, or comes down to drink from them. A brook explorer could take all eternity to say what he saw in a day. Coming back to the poets, one thing they have always distilled from New England water — from its purity, liveliness, and grateful vicissitude — is the thought of heaven. I feel the same, and if elected shall hope to find brooks or their equivalent.

Richard Wilbur has won the Pulitzer and other prizes for his books of poems, the latest of which is *The Mind Reader*. Other recent books are *Responses* (prose pieces) and *The Learned Ladies*, a translation from Molière. He is a former president of the American Academy of Arts and Letters, and lives with his wife in Cummington, Massachusetts. He is a writer-in-residence at Smith College.

ROADSIDE BROOK
LOVELL, MAINE

While driving along the west shore road around Kezar Lake, I came upon this small brook. It is one of the many tributaries that feed this popular lake. Its pine-clad shores shelter splendid summer homes (Rudy Vallee had a home near this brook early in his career). The photographer shouldn't overlook back-lighting or the foggy atmosphere of the forest when the sunrays break through the trees to illuminate a leaf-strewn brook with golden shafts of light. The yellow and red leaves are frequently beautiful in direct back-light, which renders their structures delicately translucent. Usually the necessary difference in exposure for front- and back-lighting (in this case) was one full stop.

This lake offers all the water sports. The black and white photo shows a few of the many sailboats.

Exposure, 1/10 of a second at f:16. ASA speed 64.

Men and Trees

by ARCHIBALD MacLEISH

In the villages they planted elm trees by the grassy streets for summer shade and the etching of their winter branches on the snow. When the villages grew into towns, the elm trees kept the air sweet and the winters beautiful. When the towns became cities they died.

In the country it was different. It was rock maple the farmers planted there for sugar bush in spring and firewood in winter, and, in the autumn, yellow leaves or scarlet.

On the red brick sidewalks of the old New England cities bricks are heaved still where the elms once stood. But on the country roads the autumn maples, old re-memberers, stand as they have always stood, blazing in their gentle fire. And here in the hill towns of the western counties where lost, abandoned highways wander into pine and disappear, you follow by the dwindling maples that once lined them.

They lead to cellar holes on Cricket Hill or Briar Hill where once the maples and the roofs made peace together.

There is a silence there that is New England's — only New England's of all the silences on earth.

Archibald MacLeish, when asked to send some biographical information about himself, wrote: "The essential fact is that I was born. That happened in 1892. My education was my mother, Yale, Harvard Law School, the Second Battle of the Marne, five years in Paris in the twenties, nine years writing for *Fortune*, six years as Librarian of Congress and Assistant Secretary of State in the Second World War, thirteen years as Boylston Professor (poetry) at Harvard, and a long, long love affair with my wife. A kind president gave me the Presidential Medal of Freedom; a kind academy, its gold medal for poetry; and a generous jury the National Medal for Literature."

THE BERKSHIRES MASSACHUSETTS

To me the fall foliage season in New England is a must for pictures. I usually reserve about three weeks and start up north then follow the changing of the color south. I haven't missed this colorful period for over thirty years. When I first traveled up north accommodations were easy to find, but not too good. Nowadays you have to make reservations many months ahead or you'll find yourself sleeping in your car, the village school, or some other makeshift lodging. There are actually thousands of road scenes like this one in New England. At first glance they look alike. I sent Archibald MacLeish this picture. He wrote, "It looks like and it could easily be the road past my house on the hill in Conway." Perhaps it is, for I did make it in Conway where he resides. The black and white picture is in Ashfield, next to Conway.

Exposure, 1/25 of a second at f:11. ASA speed 64.

Whistling Wings

by GEORGE HEINOLD

There is a certain breed of New Englander who, while hidden in grass-covered structures called blinds, watches many a sunrise. These men are duck hunters or waterfowlers. They endure all kinds of weather to hunt their quarry, be they black ducks, mallards, teal or bluebills.

Dawn is when ducks awaken and fly to feeding grounds. If lucky for the hunters, they will fly past their blinds in gunshot range. Or, better still, they will alight among the wooden decoys they have strung in the water close to their blinds. Sometimes flocks of twenty or more birds will alight. Then the marshlands will resound with shotgun fire.

Duck hunters take great pains in the pursuit of their sport. They spend many a long winter night repairing and painting their decoys. And then, weeks before the season opens, they build their blinds, rough structures of wooden frame covered with meadow grass. The blinds must be built before the season opens so that the ducks will get used to seeing them. They also must have boats, to set out their decoys and retrieve fallen ducks.

Because all waterfowl have keen eyesight, duck hunters dress in drab tan clothes, not the bright dress of the upland gunner. Some even go to the trouble of putting lamp black on their faces. And when the ducks fly near they crouch and remain as motionless as possible.

Because of the range that is often involved and the thickness of the duck's feathers, long-barreled, hard-hitting shotguns are used. They are loaded with heavy ammunition, number four shot, sometimes even twos. Because of the speed with which ducks fly, hunters use considerable lead when they shoot. Guns holding more than three cartridges may not be used.

Outside of hunting licenses and duck stamps, waterfowlers also contribute generously to an organization called Ducks Unlimited. The funds thus raised are used to buy and maintain breeding and nesting grounds in the Canadian provinces, where most of the ducks nest each spring and summer. Duck Unlimited has done a great deal to keep the waterfowl population from declining to dangerous levels.

Yes, waterfowlers are a dedicated breed. They give a great deal in effort and financial support to maintain their sport. Incidentally, autumn-fattened waterfowl are a gourmet's delight.

George Heinold, sixty-seven, of Killingworth, Connecticut, is a lifetime hunter and fisherman and, as one editor put it, an advanced amateur naturalist. Over the past forty years or so, he has written for *Outdoor Life, Field & Stream, Sports Afield, True, Argosy,* the *Saturday Evening Post, Ford Times, Reader's Digest,* and *Yankee.*

MADISON, CONNECTICUT

Duck hunting has been a favorite sport all over Long Island Sound since the first settlers arrived. I got up long before daybreak with this group of hunters to get to their blind, put out decoys, and hide before the ducks came flying over. They didn't come this day. I didn't even capture a colorful sunrise, but I think that at times a typical moody sunrise makes an interesting change of pace, especially when I have a few sparkling sunrises on other pages. Incidentally, the hunter in the middle of this photo is the author of the adjoining essay. This picture was taken some thirty years ago when we were working together on assignment for the Saturday Evening Post.

Nearby is Guilford, an early Colonial village which has preserved the most varied collection of authentic early houses in New England. The black and white photo is the Whitfield Stone House.

Exposure, 1/10 of a second at f:8. ASA speed 20.

Small That Is Indeed Beautiful

by JOHN KENNETH GALBRAITH

The road goes straight through Newfane, as once did the railroad, and a certain number of people do not stop. They are fugitives from justice, have their thoughts on love or they have not heard that Newfane is the loveliest village in all New England. At least the discriminating so view it.

There is some question as to the source of this beauty. Williamsburg, Virginia, not a negligible place, owes much to its restoration and somewhat less to the contrast with the sheer awfulness of the freely franchised enterprise on the way in from Richmond. Bill's garage in Newfane once had a very decent collection of destitute automobiles, but it was not bad enough to make a really great contrast, and it is run by an exceptionally obliging man and a fine mechanic. Beauty is not free.

The maples around the Newfane common and up the two side streets are a strong point. They are large and gracious, but have been badly butchered to let the power and telephone lines through. In 1975, it was my pleasure to make the address celebrating Newfane's very own bicentennial, a pleasure only slightly diluted by the knowledge that I was substituting for Spiro Agnew, who unexpectedly had become unavailable. I offered as my main hope for the next two centuries that the utility lines might all be put underground.

The Newfane common is good — spacious, smooth and symmetrical. The Civil War soldier is a man of dignity to whose plinth the heroes of later conflicts have been added. But other New England towns have good greens and dignified monuments too.

The glory of Newfane is in the architecture. The inn, the Grange Hall, the church, are all excellent and beautifully related one to the other. And in the center of all is the court house, a superbly proportioned reminder of a Wren church. Once one would have added a word for the combined hotel and jail which is across the highway at the opposite end of the common from the court house. Alas, a few years ago the hotel half was torn down. Only the jail, amiable and even beckoning but now sadly abbreviated, remains. But it is better than no jail at all, and anyone praising Newfane must also praise the few score householders and their houses. The houses are all in excellent style; all are painted a fresh white, as symmetry and good order demand. Lesser communities would have one inhabitant who would proclaim his personality by painting his house yellow with green trim. With us none does. The beauty of Newfane comes also from the beauty of its citizens.

John Kenneth Galbraith is the Paul M. Warburg Professor of Economics at Harvard. He is the author of numerous books on economic organization and fiscal policy. Among his best-known works are *The Affluent Society, The Age of Uncertainty,* and *Almost Everyone's Guide to Economics.* He lives in Cambridge and summers in Newfane, Vermont.

COURTHOUSE, NEWFANE, VERMONT

Why is it that so many of us persist in thinking that autumn is a sad season? Nature has merely fallen asleep, and her dream must be beautiful, if we are to judge by her countenance. — S. T. COLERIDGE.

Newfane stands with Woodstock as one of the most charming villages in southern Vermont. Situated on a level valley floor, banked by soft-sloping terraces, its handsome greens distinguished by town hall, church, courthouse, and a couple of old inns that serve food as good as any in all New England. It takes all of three weeks for the trees to turn, but peak color in a given area lasts only about a week — that is if you do not get high winds or heavy rain. The history of this delightful New England town is chock-full of interesting and enjoyable anecdotes. The black and white picture is of the town graveyard overlooking Newfane.

Exposure, 1/25 of a second at f:16. ASA speed 64.

Indian Summer

CONTOOCOOK RIVER NEW HAMPSHIRE

by THEODORE VRETTOS

This is New Hampshire . . . exactly as the Indian gods planted her: raw, beautiful, strong.

And this is her regal season . . . when every known color bursts from her womb and adorns the land with beauty . . . when her deep waters gush forth and send her glistening offspring down long mountain slopes to frolic and dance with these eternal stones . . . when her tender hand anoints each tree, each bush, each pebble and grain of sand.

The Indian gods still watch over her, keeping her streams pure, her air immaculate, the hem of her multicolored garment spotless.

There is no death here.

Only vibrant life.

Theodore Vrettos lives in Peabody, Massachusetts. He is the author of many short stories and articles. His novels include *Hammer on the Sea, Origen, Birds of Winter*. He is also the author of *A Shadow of Magnitude*, a nonfiction book about Lord Elgin and the Parthenon marbles.

It's not clear why our New England foliage is more colorful than anywhere else in the world. We know that cold, dry air brings out finer hues on the same tree than warm, wet air. For some still unknown reasons, during our warm Indian summer our trees are richer in reds and oranges than those in other states. New England autumns are surely the most colorful in the world. This is the north branch of the Contoocook River on Route 9 driving from Hopkinton toward Keene.

Some New Hampshire rivers are very popular for white-water canoeing in the spring, as shown in the black and white photo.

Exposure, 1/50 of a second at f:11. ASA speed 64.

They Come High

by JOHN GOULD

The American scoter, known to Mainers as the coot, was always a joke bird. Everybody remembers the recipe for cooking a coot: put an ax in the pan with the coot, and when you can stick a fork in the ax the coot is done. But 'longshore, the coot was an important meat in the old days, and lobstermen went for them in a wholesale way.

Off Jacquish Ledges, land's end at Bailey Island, was a favorite place to set tollers for coot, and some fall mornings when coot conditions were propitious, most of the island men would be out there on a killick, decoys deployed, and seldom did a coot get through the barrage that awaited him.

There are times when the view from Bailey Island is serene and lovely. There are times when seas surge against the ledges and there is no view. For coot, a quiet morning, a calm sea, a mite of overcast are ideal. We were out there on such a morning, and already most of the skiffs had some coot aboard. Wash Doughty saw some wingbeats coming, stood to wave his hat and whistle in the flock, and opened up at the right moment. He got four, but one was only wounded. Wash rowed around to pick up his birds, moved toward the cripple, and shot at it again.

The coot dove as the pellets raked the water around about, and came up a short distance beyond, as coots will. Wash push-rowed again, and the same thing happened again.

Now, why this comes to mind — off to the east'ard of Bailey Island, across the New Meadows River, is West Point. The rest of us watched Wash row across New Meadows River in pursuit of his coot, making like the Concord farmers to pause and load, and in time we could barely make him out. The coot took him across to West Point, and now we could just barely hear his shotgun when he took another crack.

He came back in the evening, long after the rest of us had come in, and the coot he finally harvested, over at West Point, was little more than a few feathers — not much left after the day-long bombardment. It was what Wash said that I liked. He said, "They come high, but I must have 'em."

That's all I know about West Point.

John Gould lives in Friendship, Maine, and is known as Mr. Maine for he's an authority on the State of Maine. He has written a weekly essay for the *Christian Science Monitor* for almost forty years, and has written eighteen books and contributed to many others.

SUNSET OVER CASCO BAY, MAINE

This picture was taken from one of the old fishing wharfs at West Point. This tiny fishing village is between Small Point and Sebasco Estates in the Fort Popham and beach area. Usually I see the possibilities of a sunset while having dinner (which means giving up the dinner or sunset — the sunset always wins). I had this location in mind for some time and I was staying at a lodge a few minutes away when I saw the sunset building up. The winter after this picture was taken a severe storm destroyed the fish house, and another picturesque part of New England was dashed away. It is very difficult to judge the correct exposure for sunsets, or to catch the height of the brilliance in any one exposure. The best method is to shoot plenty before the sun goes down over the horizon and then wait for the afterglow, which could be the most colorful moment of all.

Exposure, 1/10 of a second at f:14. ASA speed 64.

New England Classic

by JANE LANGTON

"Vermont information. What town?"

"Waits River. I want to speak to the minister of the old church there. Is there a First Parish Church in Waits River?"

(Pause) "I can't find any Waits River. Do you mean White River Junction?"

"No, no. Waits River. It's right here on the map, northeast of Barre."

"Sorry. I have no number for a church in Waits River."

"But it's right here on the —"

"Listen, you don't know how small those little towns are. They're just crossings on the road."

So I gave up trying to find out about the church in the picture. I couldn't discover, not without going there, whether the people who built it were Congregationalists or Unitarians or what. I could see only that it was a white-painted wooden box of pure outline, a solid post-and-lintel building of the same shape as the barn across the road, but with a steeple of nested boxes topped by a set of propped beams pointing straight up. It was the focal point in this classic study of a New England village, the perfect subject for the month of October on everybody's hardware-store calendar: red tree, red barn, white steeple, bright blue sky.

A thousand New England villages look like this crossing in the road. They are best seen when frost has cleared the air, when every raked pediment and corner post glistens in sharp rectilinearity, when the sugar maples have caught fire and the whole skyline burns red and yellow and blazing orange. Scattered across the northeastern corner of the United States, they are one of the great sights of the western world — red buildings to house the cattle, white ones to hold the spirit, and trees like the spirit itself abroad on the countryside.

Jane Langton writes mystery novels and children's books with New England settings.

WAITS RIVER, VERMONT

Autumn is the American Season. In Europe the leaves turn yellow or brown, and fall. Here they take fire on the trees and hang there flaming. We think this frost-fire is a portent somehow: a promise that the continent has given us. Life, too, we think, is capable of taking fire in this country; of creating beauty never seen.
— ARCHIBALD MacLEISH

This village is smack on Route 25, and is one of at least half a dozen photogenic villages nearby, especially the Corinths, of which East Corinth is the best known. This is one of the many subjects you might have to visit many times before catching the proper light. In late September and October, the Vermont landscape glows briefly but radiantly. In this scene you can observe how the scarlets, yellows, russets, and oranges have replaced the summer greens.

Exposure, 1/25 of a second at f:22. ASA speed 64.

Mellow Fruitfulness

ROADSIDE STAND
MASSACHUSETTS

by HARRY LEVIN

A small pond near Concord, not far from Thoreau's Walden, reflects the special glow of fall in Massachusetts with an inviting foretaste of Halloween or Thanksgiving. The components of this radiant still life, now displayed on a roadside stand, have been grown and planted by the successors of those embattled farmers who also had been called upon to fire the first shots for the American Revolution. But Concord has a later historical significance, somewhat better suited to its peaceful name and its fruitful terrain, once famous for grapes. During the middle years of the nineteenth century, it provided a center for the most classic flowering of American culture, which critics have sometimes called the Golden Day. What could be more golden than the day envisioned here? Hawthorne, who lived for three idyllic years in the local Old Manse, wrote about the summer squashes growing in its garden: "Art has never invented anything more graceful." One of his neighbors, who accompanied Emerson on his walks through the autumnal countryside, reported that the Sage of Concord "spoke almost with reverence of the pumpkin, saying that it had done a good deal for the settlers in early days, who would doubtless have starved without it, and that New England owed a good deal to the pumpkin." Nature's season of mellow fruitfulness, as it has been so directly captured and so tangibly presented, may well serve to remind us of our first great literary harvest.

Harry Levin, the Irving Babbitt Professor of Comparative Literature at Harvard University, has published — along with books on English and continental European literature — *The Power of Blackness: Hawthorne, Poe, Melville.*

After the enervating heat of our summer, greeting a new autumn is like coming to life again. It is as New England as pumpkin pie, maple syrup, crowds going to football games, or the roadside displays. It seems to me that roadside stands in the fall are not as prevalent as they were a few years ago. In those days, each produce stand tried to outdo the others with faces and figures made from pumpkins and other vegetables and fruit, and old clothes stuffed with straw. This wagon was almost hidden in back of the stand. I had no idea that it was there until I stopped to buy some fruit. I didn't have to add a pumpkin or rearrange anything, just got my camera and made the picture. It was the easiest Stand picture I ever made.

The black and white photo is of our daughter, Lee, and a neighbor's boy. He's now an engineer and Lee designed this book.

Exposure, 1/25 of a second at f:16. ASA speed 64.

Port Where Sea, Land and Ancient Memories Meet

by HENRY BEETLE HOUGH

This is the storied fishing port of Stonington, Connecticut, and it is also — in boats, gear, atmosphere, and even weather, for one will not miss the tinged, lowering darkness of the sky and the movement of the clouds — the likeness of other fishing ports going back anciently to the shoreside towns of history. One knows such scenes from beyond the memories of one's own lifetime because they are a visibly realized theme, early and basic, in the life of the human race.

This is where and how and in such curious symbols, mysterious to inland dwellers, landsmen find an introduction to life and labor that touches their humanity as the reach of the sea touches the coast.

Here in Stonington a boy named Ellery Thompson, having decided to leave school for a fisherman's career, received advice from his well-salted father: "Keep your feet firmly on deck, never step into a coil of rope, and stay away from the edge of the boat as much as possible." In later years Ellery wrote a book and questioned why his father, instead of saying "edge" had not used a nautical term such as "bulwarks," "rail," or "scuppers."

"It doesn't take a very vivid or poetic imagination to consider that speech as something composed of metaphors," Ellery added, "and to make it one of the soundest bits of advice any boy could have in facing any circumstance of life."

So, too, I think, we look upon the idiomatic, sometimes familiar, always expressive and stimulating, scenes of this school as metaphorical in a kind of world sense, the terms challenging, always to be sensed but never wholly interpreted or solved.

Henry Beetle Hough, born in the whaling port of New Bedford, became co-editor with his wife of the *Vineyard Gazette* on Martha's Vineyard and after almost sixty years still has an editorial status with the paper. His best known book is *Country Editor,* and among others he has written *The New England Story, The Port, To the Harbor Light,* and collaborated on *Whaling Wives,* a work of biography and the sea.

STONINGTON, CONNECTICUT

This quiet peaceful town of modest, shady streets on a narrow rocky point is close to the Rhode Island border. Its dreamy seaside lanes have large white houses where former sea captains came at last to a safe anchorage. The town still carries the atmosphere of its old whaling days. Lobster traps and fishing gear are piled on the docks at the end of side streets, all bringing back something of the old seafaring past. During the Revolutionary War and the War of 1812, the town was twice attacked from the sea. This picturesque town has loads of history and plenty of picture possibilities.

Connecticut has a beautiful coastline, but most of it is privately owned and trespassing is forbidden. Stonington, Southport, and Mystic Seaport (shown in the black and white photo) are my favorite coastal towns.

Exposure, 1/100 of a second at f:11. ASA speed 64.

WINTER

by JUSTIN KAPLAN

"Winter was always the effort to live; summer was tropical license," said Henry Adams. He claimed that "Resistance to something was the law of New England nature." Still, there comes a time even in winter when that law is suspended. We yield to the impulse to huddle, to be enclosed, private, and internal, to enjoy a time of abeyance while the natural world outside also awaits the slow, implicit process of renewal. The long winter will somehow come to an end and spring will take us by surprise, as it always does. Meanwhile, looking outward over the few tracks in the snow, we have days and nights enough to consider what lies between the fire and the altar.

Justin Kaplan lives in Cambridge, Massachusetts. He is the author of, among other books, the Pulitzer Prize–winning *Mr. Clemens and Mark Twain* and of a forthcoming biography of Walt Whitman.

WEST DUMMERSTON, VERMONT

This small peaceful village is one of many in Vermont that is very photogenic. Once again we had to turn the lights on in the church, without the illumination you just wouldn't have a picture. West Dummerston is on Route 30 about ten miles north of Brattleboro. This winding road runs along the West River and goes through Newfane, Townshend, and Jamaica, all picturesque towns.

Exposure, about 20 seconds at f:16. ASA speed 64.

Common Land

by JOHN UPDIKE

We seek, Americans, to inhale freedom, and the air is here, in these communities of houses built one by one, along roads whose curves were derived from the lay of the land. Predating the merciless grid that seized Manhattan and possessed the vast Midwest, New England towns have each at their center an irregular heart of open grass, vestige of the Puritan common, holding, perhaps, a village pump, a weathered monument, a surviving elm. In Rowley, a vacant triangle beside Route 1A that as December narrows becomes suddenly alive with whirling dervishes of Christmas lights. Ipswich has two hearts — the teardrop-shaped Meetinghouse Green at the old center, now overburdened by its sprawling modern meetinghouse, and the elongate, gracious South Green, since the 1830s made Arcadian by the backdrop of a Doric-columned church that in one cold recent night burned to its granite foundation. Away from the sea, the old greens merge with the wider lawns and what fields remain of New England's agriculture. The white house here was once a farmhouse. Once there would have been determined paths beaten to the pump through this cold blue purity of snow.

In New Hampshire, the sheds of the houses reach backward to the barns, to afford the busy occupants roofed passage, and one feels the intensity of winter in such actively sheltering shapes. Here, in regions becoming suburban to Boston, the land is allowed to sleep, and the clapboard saltboxes remember summer as they accept the weak sun on their sides. Wires trace a secret traffic in heat and light, and no doubt feed that cool new hearthfire, the television set. The houses seem to enjoy no very intrinsic relation to the greens in their midst; they send out only an occasional band of children to inherit with casual play the spaces originally set aside for pasturage and militia drills. But the idea, of land held in common, as — more than park or playground — part of a manifest, workaday covenant with the Bestower of a new continent, has permanently imprinted the maps of these towns, and lengthens the perspectives of those who live within them.

John Updike, born in Pennsylvania in 1932, has lived in Massachusetts for over twenty years. He is the author of nine novels and numerous collections of poetry, short fiction, and essays. His present home is in Georgetown, ten minutes from the site of this photograph.

WEST NEWBURY, MASSACHUSETTS

This peaceful little settlement with its small green or common hasn't changed in many years. We made the color and black and white photos some thirty years ago, and in revisiting this village recently I feel that time has passed it by. Believe me, that's all to the good! The color picture was made in late afternoon; you can just about see the last rays of the sun on the houses. This is a very old picture and was made on Kodachrome film, which was much more permanent than the newer Ektachrome film. Regrettably, Kodak stopped selling the large professional sizes of Kodachrome when they brought out their self-processing Ektachrome.

Exposure, 1/10 of a second at f:8. ASA speed 20.

A Fleece of Fire and Amethyst

by ROBERT TAYLOR

Winter is Viking weather. Pemaquid — in Algonquin a "long point of land" — has harbored the dragon prows of Norsemen, English fishing smacks, Coast Guard cutters, rumrunners and pirate hulls of every description. This was a busy seaport decades before the Pilgrims landed in Plymouth to be astonished by English-speaking Samoset and Squanto. As Maine's first permanent settlement, England's vulnerable outpost on the North American continent, Pemaquid typifies the truly transatlantic community where cultures overlap and intermingle.

Colonial Pemaquid, however, belongs to summer, lobelias and lobster buoys, to its sparkling cove and ring of cottages. The winter summons forth an older, more solitary spirit. The landscape turns northern, fierce, aboriginal; the sea flares; the inky pilings of a pier sink into the spruce-cold night. The last rays of sunset strike a ragged crust of ice. Through the blue hush echoes possible sound. The mewling of a gull, chink of metal, approaching voices of strangers? So might Viking raiders, frozen in defensible harbors, sense their isolation. Perhaps, though, while ice-flecked tides absorbed the briefest of sunsets, the northern dusk bore memory, as it often does with sailors, toward distant fjords and farms.

And what of primeval men and women who felt the same magic? The first crossing of their Eastern Ocean started from inlets like this — Eskimos and Indians who launched giant bark canoes and skin boats, paddling across sun-streaked waters, ultimately gaining an unknown shore beyond the margin of recorded history.

Robert Taylor is art editor of the Boston *Globe,* a novelist, and professor of English at Wheaton College in Norton, Massachusetts.

SUNSET OVER PEMAQUID AND JOHNS BAY, MAINE

What a pageantry of history has sailed in this bay. Explorers, Indians, pirate raiders, French conquerors. In 1605, Pemaquid was already an old settlement. Captain John Smith explored this territory in 1614. There were probably trading settlements at both Pemaquid and Monhegan from the beginning of the sixteenth century. This section of Maine has engrossing history. Next to Captain Kidd, probably no Maine water's pirate was more famous than Dixey Bull. In 1632 he sailed into Pemaquid, sacked the trading post and carried away $2500 in booty. I made this sunset on a cold, cold late afternoon. This is a very lonely community in the winter. The deserted pier in the background is quite different in the summer, when tourists can have live lobsters boiled there.

The black and white photo is of Pemaquid Point light.

Exposure, 1/50 of a second at f:8. ASA speed 64.

Snug Boat, Snug Harbor

by WILLIAM F. BUCKLEY, JR.

I hope the Freudians haven't already thought of it, but it does occur to me that one of the mysterious attractions of boating is the snugness of the experience, perfectly caught here at two levels. First the little boats themselves, only just big enough for one or two hands, the doghouse adding to the sense of refuge. And then the little harbor, protected on all sides from the wind, with fore and aft mooring lines to guard against a clearly aggressive current. The threatening snow and ice in the foreground and the menacing winter blue in the background dramatize the little safety to be found in the little vessels. The same idea that animates the hearth, making it central to the kind of coziness that distinguishes the home from the hectic commerce of outdoor life, is a key to understanding a boat, and the privations people submit to in order to live in boats and maintain them. It is an experience without appeal to some people, but then music leaves some otherwise sensitive people untouched. John Kenneth Galbraith has never understood the attractions of boating which, as I once remarked, makes it surprising that he has not recommended a law making boating compulsory. But if that appeal is not comprehensive, it is universal, and the pulse quickens on seeing something as evocative as this winter scene, caught so perfectly by the photographer, who understands the moods of New England, and the spiritual reach of the little sanctuaries pictured here.

William F. Buckley, Jr., is one of the most distinguished writers in the country, noted not merely for the elegance of his writing style, but for his talent as a debater and, in *The National Review*, which he edits, an apologist for conservative political philosophy. His literary talents range far beyond politics. His two novels — *Saving the Queen* and *Stained Glass* — have been best sellers, and his book *Airborne*, dealing with his cruising years as a yachtsman, has the dimension of a nautical classic. His home is in Stamford, Connecticut.

ROCKPORT, MASSACHUSETTS

The fish house at the left is the most photographed and painted scene in North America and is known to artists the country over as Motif Number One. When I made this many years ago (this is my favorite Rockport picture out of many hundreds) you couldn't foresee the Great Blizzard of '78, which struck furiously on February seventh, and reduced the beloved fisherman's shack to a pile of rubble! While saddened by the loss of the town's famous landmark, Rockporters immediately established a rebuilding committee and an exact replica was erected. It is undisputably the most photographed and painted subject in New England. I like Cape Ann in all its moods and seasons, but most of all in the winter.

Exposure, 1/10 of a second at f:8. ASA speed 20.

Uphill and Cross Country

by MARIA VON TRAPP

In olden days one didn't see this very often; a group of people obviously on a hike on skis. In olden days one used to drive to "the mountain." First, one had to find a parking place. Then one walked a few minutes to join the line moving slowly to the chair lift. That could take from fifteen to twenty minutes. On the chair lift for another fifteen to twenty minutes one spent the last bit of warmth in one's body and arrived frozen stiff. One then had to take time in the hut to thaw. And then with renewed vigor one went down a steep trail, first in a fifteen-minute run and then racing one's self in ten minutes.

Now look at the picture: a group of girls on skis, hiking happily through the countryside, stopping from time to time to enjoy the view, feeling content, happy, and warm — because there was no standing in line and freezing on the chair lift. It is known as cross-country skiing or ski touring.

About ten years ago this was mostly a fad in some northern colleges. Not many people outside of the colleges did it because heavy downhill skis didn't lend themselves to easy walking. Then cross-country skis emerged: light, narrow skis without metal strips, fitting the slipper like shoes.

Many people in the North however picked it up privately and, finally, my son, Johannes von Trapp, brought it out in the open. He knew that cross-country skiing was always a way of locomotion in Scandinavia. His Norwegian roommate in college showed him pictures from home very similar to the picture here. So Johannes advertised in Norwegian newspapers for an instructor for cross-country skiing, and hired Per Soerle. A new era began at the Trapp Family Lodge in Stowe, Vermont.

A large garage was made into a ski shop where all the necessary articles were on sale and at the desk the guests could ask for either a private lesson with Per or for a group lesson. There was happy excitement throughout the whole winter and at the end Johannes counted 500 participants and he and Per were quite satisfied. The old ski shop was destroyed by fire, and a bigger and better one with two stories, show rooms, a large warming-up area, big picture windows and — the show-piece of it all — a fireplace built by Johannes's brother, Werner, was built.

Johannes, by profession a forester, has with a forester's eye built over sixty miles of trails into our woodlands. And the idea of cross-country skiing has grown so much that now on a weekend in winter over 1000 people enjoy themselves here.

Baroness Maria Augusta von Trapp of Stowe, Vermont, is a legendary figure, the heroine of *The Sound of Music*. She is also the author of half a dozen books, and she founded her famous ski lodge. She is presently working on the *Trapp Family Lodge Cook Book*.

94

TOLL ROAD
MOUNT MANSFIELD, VERMONT

It's that magic time of the year when Mother Nature swirls her white mantle over the countryside, covering the earth with sparkling snow. Overnight the world undergoes a metamorphosis — fir trees, laden with freshly fallen snow, take on magical forms. This picture was one that I made for the Girl Scout calendar. It was a very, very cold day and the young girls were as uncomfortable as I. You need to make the most of side- or back-lighting with sun and snow. This reveals the beautiful texture of the snow and gives invaluable modeling that's always missing in front-lighted snow pictures. Remember that snow is a fantastically effective reflector that will bounce enough light into the darkest shadows.

The snow in northern New England can get very deep and, as shown in the black and white photo, one needs skis or snowshoes to get off the beaten trails.

Exposure, 1/25 of a second at f:24. ASA speed 64.

The Massachusetts State House

by DOUGLASS SHAND TUCCI

The Massachusetts State House has presided over Beacon Hill and Boston Common since 1798. It does so with a singular distinction. "High in the air, poised in the right place" — in Henry James's words — its burnished gold dome is not just Boston's landmark; it is the most famous version of the architectural form that for two hundred years has symbolized American democracy. This is ironic. For many decades after its erection, the Massachusetts State House was — as Sinclair Hitchings and Catherine H. Farlow have written in their excellent history of the capitol — "the most prominent building in the United States"; of all American landmarks it was the first and most complete architectural expression of the newly independent country. Yet its architect, Charles Bulfinch, took his inspiration from the river-front pavilion of Somerset House in London; striking evidence that although it led the political revolt of the colonies, Boston sought no cultural declaration of independence. This is perhaps why Lord Coleridge, sometime chief justice of England, found the State House so admirable, pronouncing it in 1883 "the most beautiful building in the country."

The State House is not, however, in any sense of the word, a copy. It was precisely the genius of Bulfinch, who was only thirty-four when what is perhaps his masterpiece was completed, that he endowed the building with a lighter and more refined character that is very much his own work. And although the various later additions (including the white marble and granite wings visible in the photograph, built between 1914 and 1917) have not been universally liked, the Bulfinch building itself is still greatly admired today. Just recently Professor William Pierson, in his book *The Colonial and Neo-Classical Styles,* remarked of the main-story arcade that the piers and arches formed "one of the most expressive and lovely passages in American architecture."

The men and events associated with the State House also command attention. The cornerstone was laid by Sam Adams and Paul Revere. Here, for example, La-Fayette was received in 1825, when he addressed the Greate and General Court, as the Massachusetts Legislature is still called. Here too, in 1961, John Fitzgerald Kennedy spoke to the legislature. And it was a keen sense of place that moved him to quote that day John Winthrop's words of 1630, the year Boston was founded: "we shall be as a city upon a hill, the eyes of all people are upon us."

Since his graduation from Harvard College in 1972 Douglass Shand Tucci has written and lectured widely on Boston cultural history. He now teaches the subject at Harvard, where he is also a member of the Senior Common Room of Eliot House. His most recent book, *Built in Boston, City and Suburb,* was published by Little, Brown in 1978.

MASSACHUSETTS STATE HOUSE

The Massachusetts State House is handsomely situated on the highest point in downtown Boston — Beacon Hill. Once this section was mostly pasturage and orchard with a scattering of handsome estates. This Bulfinch designed building overlooks the Common. Among the first things the settlers of Boston did was to set aside certain lands for common pasturage and a common training ground. It was to be forever a place for all to take pleasure. Generations of children have played here, from Puritan children with kite, marbles, hoops, and sleds to today's urchins shrieking in the Frog Pond. The greatest of colonial military parades and musters took place on the Common. From here the British troops marched to Lexington, Concord, and Bunker Hill.

The black and white photo shows Major General "Fighting Joe" Hooker of Civil War fame, whose statue is in front of the State House.

Exposure, 1/25 of a second at f:22. ASA speed 64.

The Covered Bridge

by JOHN DEEDY

They were called kissing bridges, and indeed many's the kiss that was stolen in the darkened interiors of covered bridges. But covered bridges were more than convenient trysting spots for couples passing through in one-horse shays. They represented a triumph of local craftsmanship — and a surge of the spirit. Author and artist Eric Sloane says that the covered bridge was to the nineteenth century what the barn was to the eighteenth. In the sense that the covered bridge reflected the impulse to forge rivers, shift roots, and expand horizons, he is correct. But the covered bridge was also an expression of community, an eagerness to be closer to the folks "on the other side." It is not surprising, therefore, that the covered bridge was often a meeting place for groups of citizens.

Accustomed as we are now to open bridges, the covered bridge, in retrospect, seems something of an anomaly. Its sideboards and roof appear superfluous, almost an invitation to winds to topple the structure. But that covering had very practical purposes — still does, for surviving covered bridges. The covering added strength to the structure, making the bridge in fact more solid; and it kept rain and snow away from the floor planks and the support joints, thus protecting vital woods against rot.

As a boy, I traveled through many covered bridges during two glorious Vermont summers. It was always an exhilarating experience. I'd make a wish — for covered bridges are wishing bridges, too — usually that I would come back one day to Vermont. I did. For four years I drove two of my children back and forth between New York City and a college near Burlington. We traveled on those sleek super-highways that sweep you around mountains, cities, and towns, affording you a view of everything except people. On one of the early trips I spied a covered bridge somewhere north of White River Junction. The highway cut along a mountain ridge and there, perhaps two hundred feet below, was the covered bridge negotiating a slow, stony Green Mountain stream. By craning my neck as the car sped along at fifty-five or sixty miles per hour, I could glimpse the covered bridge for all of several seconds. It was a thrilling sight. Someday, I said to myself, I'll seek out the exit to that covered bridge, and drive or walk through it. Alas, there was never time. I never got to make one last wish.

John Deedy returned to New England in 1978 after twenty years in Pittsburgh and New York as an editor and author of books, including *Literary Places: A Guided Pilgrimage, New York and New England*. He now lives in Rockport, Massachusetts, where he overlooks the water and dreams of New York.

CHISTLEVILLE BRIDGE, VERMONT

High over the Roaring Branch in Sunderland is my favorite covered bridge. Shortly after taking this picture I fell through the snow and ice into almost hip-deep cooold water. Fortunately, my camera and tripod didn't go in with me, but I did have trouble getting out through the deep snow and ice breaking around me. The black and white photo of me fishing from about the same location is one of many that Claire took over the years whenever we couldn't find a real fisherman to be in the pictures. I always used a stone on the end of the line to bend the rod a bit. One day in the Berkshires, Claire had me "fishing" when a game warden called from the shore inquiring if I had a fishing permit, I yelled back "No"! He commanded me to come right out, which I did, carefully keeping the stone on the line. When he saw what I used for bait, he was very disappointed, but a can of cold beer cooled him off.

Exposure, 1/25 of a second at f:22. ASA speed 64.

The Two Ends of Winter

by DON STONE

When first viewing this photograph of Amherst, New Hampshire, my thoughts immediately went back to my childhood and the long but beautiful winters spent living here in New England with my grandmother. About heading home after a hard day of sledding, usually late for that always waiting supper on the back of the old Glenwood C, with frozen corduroys whistling in the stillness of the crisp early evening. Grandmother always said that she enjoyed wintertime — when her backyard looked as clean as her neighbor's — the best.

My love for the winter is still as strong as it was back then, but now it's more for artistic reasons, when I can enjoy painting the two ends of winter. The late fall and with it the first snow! Who could ever forget that thrilling sensation when the earth is changed from its bedding of sienna and umbers to a pure blanket of white. Then finally spring when the earth begins to push its way through the melting snow creating the beautiful combination of the abstract patterns along with those ever present realistic forms.

Here in this marvelous photograph Mr. Griffin has done just that. He has captured on film what I would have liked to have portrayed with brush and paint; that unhurried life of New England, almost timeless in a way, showing no cars or costumed covered figures to give us a hint of the date. It could have been back when grandmother was a child or it could have been just yesterday.

Don Stone, a native New Englander who lives in Ogunquit, Maine, was educated at Vesper George School of Art in Boston, Massachusetts. He is an associate member of the National Academy of Design and holds full membership in the American Watercolor Society. He is represented by numerous galleries and art associations both in this country and abroad.

AMHERST, NEW HAMPSHIRE

Not many tourists visit Amherst since it's a couple of miles off the traveled roads and offers no accommodations. It is really a charming town and sits in dignity around a long pear-shaped common, dominated by the tall, graceful steeple of the old white meetinghouse. In this photo the meetinghouse is reflected in the flooded skating rink in the common; it was taken late in March. Amherst and its nearby towns and villages convey New England in the most peaceful of settings.

The black and white photo shows that late March thaws were not very pretty up on the back country roads thirty-five years ago. We often got mired in deep mud while trying to photograph maple sugaring. This picture was taken way up in Vermont and our car was the last car out of this area for almost a month.

Exposure, 1/25 of a second at f:16. ASA speed 64.

A Dark Silent Haven

by ERICA WILSON

How many holidays do I remember, when we would take that long drive from the city, playing ghost and geography with the children till at last the familiar curve in the road loomed up through the swirling snow. After three or four tries we'd finally rush up the driveway, slipping and swaying on the ferocious black ice, lying all un-suspected under its innocent swan's down coverlet of fluffy white.

What a haven was the dark silent house on nights like this, waiting for the dash of children, the clatter of skis and the extra inside snowfall as our dog shook himself gratefully, each long-haired paw encased in a large white snowball. Then later, si-lence would settle again with nothing to break it but the occasional crackle of logs in the fireplace. The peaceful weekend had begun — the time for reading, writing, stitching and drawing without interruption.

Threading my way around the world, with needlework inspiration everywhere, the little house would fade away to become an English manor, its long galleries peo-pled with Elizabethan ladies, or to Peking's Forbidden City where the Dowager Em-press, in silken embroidered robes, would be carried in a sedan chair through the gardens of her summer palace, or to a sod house in Kansas, where a quilter would ride out a five-day dust storm — her stitching helping to preserve her sanity.

Unheeded, the clock would quietly tick away the time till dawn crept through the frosty windows. Only moments later, it seemed, came the shrill whistle of the kettle and, "Get up, all you lazy bones, it's time to go skiing!" The rush of dogs and children would send papers flying and put all book writing to an end for good . . . another day had begun. What was that I said about a peaceful, uninterrupted week-end?! Ah, well, I can always continue on the ski lift.

Erica Wilson is an expert needleworker and author of eight books and "Needleplay," a syndi-cated column on needlework; star of two TV shows on needlework; and organizer of Erica Wilson Needlework Seminar Tours. Among her best-selling needlework books are: *Crewel Embroidery, Fun with Crewel, Erica Wilson's Embroidery Book, Needleplay,* and *More Needleplay.*

PROSPER, VERMONT

The first flake floats downward and soon the gray still-ness is filled with the soft lazy slants of the early snow. Hills whiten and the trees are webbed with softness. The snow's gentle curtain drifts, smoothing, wrapping, tucking the land into sleep. When I made this picture a few years ago, the farm was owned by Maurice Sawyer (he has sold it since). With the exception of his old brick farmhouse, all his barns and outbuildings were painted a deep barn red with white trim. The farm had a heavy grove of large sugar maples with a red sugar house among them. I have taken pictures up here in all the seasons.

Claire's picture shows Maurice taking his beagles out on his daily trip for rabbits.

Exposure, 1/10 of a second at f:22. ASA speed 64.

Louisburg Square

by JOHN LEGGETT

Looking into Louisburg Square from the Mount Vernon Street corner, as Arthur Griffin's viewfinder does here, drops me through several time warps, for this was the scene from the window of the house I rented in the summer of 1950, when I first came to Boston to work for the venerable publisher Houghton Mifflin.

That the scene looked familiar at first glance was accounted for by its having been used as the setting for *Berkeley Square,* even though that marvelously romantic Leslie Howard film was set in London. Incidentally, it was about a time warp.

The handsome, iron fence recalls Frank Hatch Sr.'s song about Louisburg Square and the Boston maiden who would rather be inside that fence, insulated from elbow-rubbing, than anyplace she can think of, *including* the Athenaeum.

Just across the Square, at Number 18, my boss Lovell Thompson lived for a while, and his dinner parties there, welcoming author guests, had a truly Dickensian warmth. It seems that most of my recollections of the Square are Lucullan ones. In the basement apartment of a house on the same side, Rosalind Wilson gave a party at which she served perforated peaches in glasses of champagne, and Edwin O'Connor entertained us with his stories about James Michael Curley, stories that were to be the heart of *The Last Hurrah.*

A few doors along Mount Vernon Street stands the Club of Odd Volumes where the principal event of my first publishing year took place, Houghton's reception for its most celebrated author, Winston Churchill.

Just up Pinckney Street, at the far side of the Square, was Laurette Murdoch's studio where many of us met for her Thursday luncheons. Over wine, omelettes and salad, we talked shop and learned what was really important about publishing.

Louisburg Square only seems unchanged. For me it is not just memories of past pleasures but it also starts thoughts of present and future ones.

John Leggett lives in Manchester, Massachusetts, now largely in the summer, for he is director of the University of Iowa Writers' Workshop. He is author of the novels *Wilder Stone, The Gloucester Branch,* and *Who Took the Gold Away; Ross and Tom,* a biography of Ross Lockridge and Thomas Heggen; and, most recently, the novel *Gulliver House.*

LOUISBURG SQUARE
BOSTON, MASSACHUSETTS

This beautiful square is the epitome of Beacon Hill. Here Christmas Eve is celebrated with such joyful profusion of candles and carols that even the most skeptical can become a believer. The green belongs to the twenty-two proprietors of the Square. Louisa May Alcott lived at Number 11. Jenny Lind was married at Number 20. William Dean Howells wrote his novels at Number 4. It is the most photogenic square in Boston but also the most difficult to photograph, mainly because of the many autos parked around the green. I got this lonely photo early one Sunday morning quite a few years ago and managed to avoid all but one auto. I doubt if I could ever do it again!

Exposure, 1/25 of a second at f:11. ASA speed 20.

First Love

by LEE WINSLOW COURT

Like many before me, my love affair with northern New England began early in my life, shortly after I completed my formal art training.

First in the area of Peacham, Wells River, and Corinth, Vermont; later I discovered Mount Mansfield encircled by picturesque valleys, among them the universal favorite, Pleasant Valley. I finally settled in the West River Valley in southern Vermont among the mountains, streams and brooks that make up this remarkably poetic country.

The splendor of her seasons, the tenacity of her landscape and the indomitable inhabitants have given quiet strength to me in my continuing endeavor to capture the spirit of New England. Robert Frost talked of "the edge of the wood," "the less-traveled road," "the people as they are." How I wish I could paint Vermont as he saw it with its harmony of color arrangements, reproduce the music that is in the air, record the acceptance of each dramatic weather change. Always, her challenging deep snow is a constant inspiration to my work.

However no love affair ever runs smoothly. A real crusher occurred one fall while painting with friends in Waterville, New Hampshire. My subject included a schoolhouse lying in the near distance; at recess the kids came bounding out, spotted us on the side hill, then scampered up to see what we were doing. One youngster raced ahead of the rest, took a look at my canvas, the result of two hours' work, cupped his hands and shouted, " 'Tain't worth it kids, don't bother!"

Yet my growing love for the seasonal revelations of this beautiful northeast country never faltered and I think it explains why great poets, musicians, artists and writers of the past, as well as those of the future, are lured as I am to New England.

Lee Court has been long recognized as a foremost chronicler of New England snowscapes and Maine marinas. His geographic interests recently expanded to the awesome Antarctic, Ireland, the Canadian Rockies and, in 1978, the formidable Arctic. His works are in many permanent collections including the National Archives, Washington, D.C. Among his awards is the French Legion of Honor. Mr. Court maintains a studio on Monhegan Island, Maine, and resides in West Townshend, Vermont.

MOUNT MANSFIELD, VERMONT

The mass of Mount Mansfield fills the valley ahead. This late afternoon scene was taken on the Pleasant Valley Road close to Cambridge and Jeffersonville and shows the northwest face of this majestic mountain in all its splendor. The countryside is very open here, and is one of the finest natural settings in the state. Winters in Vermont are not as severe as imagined. They are fairly comfortable and very exhilarating. Immaculate white landscapes, snow-covered villages and gleaming ski slopes are always accessible, due to a system of road plowing and sanding superior to those in most states. The two kids coming home from the country store help this lonely cold scene. The most dramatic snow pictures are made in late afternoon. At that time you can capture beautiful blue and purple shadows.

The black and white photo was shot in Windham.

Exposure, 1/25 of a second at f:16. ASA speed 64.

The Old North Bridge

by WALTER D. EDMONDS

Bridges have always had a special hold on man's imagination, but as bridges go this seems a small and insignificant contraption, arching a narrow stream as it did two hundred years ago. It is not, of course, that span, which also was built of wood, but a replica as accurate as men could make it — narrow enough to be called a footbridge, but wide enough in that earlier time to offer passage to a cart and a careful horse. Yet today it is a symbol of hope to men all over this earth.

A friend, like myself a native of upstate New York, who was making a trip around the world some twenty years ago, was asked in country after country, by people of widely different walks of life, "Have you been to see the bridge?" It took her some time to realize that they did not mean the George Washington Bridge in New York or the Golden Gate Bridge in San Francisco: they meant this simple wooden structure in Concord, Massachusetts. And many of them could, and did, often in halting, even broken, English, repeat to her that here ". . . the embattled farmers stood/And fired the shot heard round the world."

Walter D. Edmonds was born in Boonville, New York, and has been a resident of Concord, Massachusetts, for many years. He is the author of many books and the recipient of the National Book Award for *Bert Breen's Barn* in 1976.

OLD NORTH BRIDGE
CONCORD, MASSACHUSETTS

I suppose that the George Washington Bridge is more impressive, the Golden Gate Bridge more glamorous, but to me this wooden bridge over the Concord River is the most valuable bridge in America. This is the replica of the historic "rude bridge that arched the flood." The famous bronze statue of the Minuteman leaving his plow can be seen in the background and also in the black and white photo. Nearby Lexington has its Minuteman statue too; both towns are a mecca for photographers.

Exposure, 1/25 of a second at f:24. ASA speed 64.

Light from a Meetinghouse Window

by PAUL BROOKS

The beauty of the old New England village has not come about by chance. It is an enduring reminder of an earlier way of living. It reflects a sense of community, at the center of which stood the meetinghouse, or "house of worship." Here was the focus of social as well as spiritual life. And here the early colonists acquired at town meetings the political skills later so valuable when they were called upon to govern themselves.

These old villages no longer seem merely "quaint" when we think of them in terms of modern town planning. The first settlers brought with them a sense of husbandry developed over the centuries on an island too small for ruthless exploitation. Title to land, as well as the location of dwellings and farms, was closely controlled by the proprietors, and later by the selectmen. John Winthrop was looking to the future when he recommended the setting aside of ample areas "for newcomers and for commons," and when he visualized the growth of the colony in terms of new towns to be founded in the wilderness, as opposed to what we now call "urban sprawl."

Not all the light that shone from the meetinghouse, however, was benign. New England was to be a "garden of the saints," snugly protected from untamed wilderness and alien creeds. For it was not the principle of religious freedom but, rather, the freedom to practice their own religion, that drove the Puritans to cross the ocean. As for the wilderness, they saw it as something to be "subdued," on the assumption that anything not immediately useful to man was inherently evil. The Indians who lived there had no real claim to it. "They ramble over much land," wrote Winthrop, "without title or property."

However they acquired their rights of possession, the new owners demonstrated an instinctive feeling for beauty in planning their towns in harmony with the land, and a sense of stewardship that abides in many communities to this day. Here in Lower Waterford, Vermont, known as White Village, the meetinghouse and the library stand together as living links with the past.

Editor-in-chief of Houghton Mifflin Company for many years, Paul Brooks retired early to devote full time to his writing. Beginning with *Roadless Area* (1964), he has written four books, the latest of which is *The View from Lincoln Hill: Man and the Land in a New England Town.*

LOWER WATERFORD, VERMONT

Winter in New England! It's everywhere. Gaze out a window at a row of snow covered fence pickets and trees glistening in ice. Walk along a country road and hear the crunch of snow under your boots. Shovel a path and feel the spray of snow, blown by the north winds, melt against your warm cheeks. This peaceful village right across the New Hampshire state line is one of the best for night photos. All the homes are painted white. Therefore the name "The White Village." Don't expect to find the church illuminated. We had to get the keys and turn on the lights. To capture blue skies in night pictures you have to take the picture at dusk. It has to be dark enough to have the lights show and at the same time have a blue sky. If you wait too long the sky will photograph black. When in doubt, take the professional's theory that film is actually inexpensive (what did it cost you to get there?) and bracket your meter reading.

Exposure, about 30 seconds at f:22. ASA speed 64.